The Resurrection Report

The Resurrection Report

WILLIAM PROCTOR
Best-selling Author and former *New York Daily Times* Reporter

BROADMAN
& HOLMAN
PUBLISHERS

Nashville, Tennessee

0-8054-6372-0

Published by Broadman & Holman Publishers, Nashville, Tennessee
Acquisitions and Development Editor: Leonard Goss
Page Design and Typography: Anderson Thomas Design,
Nashville, Tennessee

Dewey Decimal Classification: 232.97
Subject Heading: JESUS CHRIST—RESURRECTION
Library of Congress Card Catalog Number: 97-33608

Unless otherwise stated, all Scripture citation is from the Holy Bible, New International Version, copyright © 1973, 1978, 1984 by International Bible Sociey. Other passages are marked NASB, the New American Standard Bible, © the Lockman Foundation, 1960, 1962, 1963, 1968, 1971, 1972, 1973, 1975, 1977; used by permission.

Library of Congress Cataloging-in-Publication Data
Proctor, William.
  The Resurrection report : a journalist investigates the most debated event in history / William Proctor.
         p.   cm.
  Includes bibliographical references and index.
  ISBN 0-8054-6372-0 (pbk.)
  1. Jesus Christ—Resurrection. 2. Jesus Christ—Resurrection—Biblical teaching. 3. N. T. Gospels—Evidences, authority, etc. I. Title.
BT481.P76 1998
232.9'7—dc21
                                                        97-33608
                                                        CIP

98 99 00 01 02 5 4 3 2 1

DEDICATION

To Pam and Mike,

whose hard questions in family discussions have
raised important issues about the Resurrection—
and helped me discover some answers.

CONTENTS

PART 1

The Search for the Greatest News Story

CHAPTER 1

The Greatest News Story of All Time?

News reporters are a hard-boiled, cynical lot. They make their home on the underside of life, where they learn to believe little and expect the worst.

Reporters like nothing better than to poke holes in pompous public figures and phony-sounding "facts." Hypocrisy and lies are their meat and potatoes. Skepticism is their spice of life. So deeply ingrained is their distrust in human nature that they are surprised—and may even be stunned—when they encounter a politician, business mogul, or spiritual guru who actually does more good than evil.

Reporters see so much lying, cheating, and violence every working day that they have little trouble believing in original sin—even if they don't call it that. And you can bet most of them don't call it sin. Poll after poll has shown that big-city reporters simply don't place as high a priority on God and religion as the general public.

But even though today's working press operates in a near spiritual vacuum, where suspicion and disbelief abound, there are occasional glimmers of faith and hope. A reporter may light a good-news candle—perhaps through an in-depth personality profile, a holiday feature, or maybe a heart-tugging human-interest story about a comeback from a near-fatal injury. In fact, editors are always on the lookout for the personal or human-interest angle because they know that warmth and inspiration sell.

Still, most members of the press are not actively digging for soul-searching, spiritually edifying subjects. Their ambitions are considerably more earthbound, with a marked preference for corruption, public immorality, and mayhem. The bad news is almost always chosen over the good.

I can speak with some authority about journalists because I am one. As a former legal and criminal courts reporter for the New York *Daily News*, I spent almost every waking hour exploring the rotten innards of the Big Apple. My main beat was the Manhattan district attorney's office, where my daily fare included Mafia hits, loan shark extortion, police corruption, and practically every other variety of high-profile crime.

Like my competitors at the *Times*, the *Post*, and the Associated Press, I knew that the best way to get high-profile play in the paper was first to find some major public scandal, shocking murder, or other egregious threat to the general welfare. Then, in my write-up, I would make the bad news seem even worse by giving my "lead" (first sentence or two) a wickedly sensational spin.

Yet even as journalists search for something publishable amid the dregs and dross of life, most also keep a sharp and critical eye out for the truly memorable story—the "Big One" that has the potential to out-shine all others and dominate the front page. For a reporter, finding such a news nugget is the journalistic equivalent of discovering the Holy Grail. This sort of story has the power to grab the banner headline of a tabloid, or to lead off a TV report, or in the most dramatic cases, to win a prize and perhaps even make history.

Although I switched from the business of daily news gathering to journalistic nonfiction book writing more than twenty years ago, I still find myself looking for the "Big One." When my own imagination takes flight above the humdrum of daily writing and research, I try to picture the *ultimate* story: the report with the power to make page one, *and* define a reporter's career, *and* maybe even qualify as the greatest story of all time, bar none.

Whenever I muse along these lines, one story idea dominates my thinking above all others: the Resurrection of Jesus Christ. But what can a hard-bitten reporter possibly have to say about such a decisive historical event as the Resurrection?

What Can a Reporter Bring to the Resurrection?

The Resurrection has been evaluated, interpreted, and dissected by experts from many disciplines. Theologians, Bible scholars, and historians have devoted countless hours to this topic, as have preachers, inspirational writers, poets, novelists, and even scientists—who may speculate on possible atomic or chemical reactions that may have occurred in Christ's tomb on that first Easter morning.

Yet in the search for the true meaning of the Resurrection, one area of expertise—perhaps the most obvious—has been overlooked: the field of journalism.

It seems rather remarkable that the standards and tools of the news reporter have never been applied to the Easter event. After all, the New

Testament accounts, on their face, appear to be what the average lay person today would regard as a kind of news story.

Like modern-day journalists, the New Testament writers reported occurrences and encounters involving relatively recent or ongoing current events—such as the resurrection itself, Jesus' appearances, and the subsequent spreading of the new Christian religion. Like reporters today—and unlike most historians—the resurrection reporters wrote soon after the events they described. The first New Testament reports on the Resurrection were probably put into finished form beginning about A.D. 45–55 or fifteen to twenty-five years after the Resurrection occurred. (The year for the Resurrection, which I have chosen in this book, has been estimated by many scholars to be A.D. 30.) By about A.D. 85–90, all of the accounts had probably been written and published.

As you might expect, these written accounts were circulating while many of the participants could still read them. Paul noted in A.D. 55–56, for instance, in his first letter to the church at Corinth (15:6), that most of the more than five hundred witnesses who saw the resurrected Christ on one particular occasion were still alive.

Also, the techniques and sources the reporters used in putting together the resurrection narratives are similar to the approach used in modern-day news media. It is clear, for instance, that the reports are based on eyewitness interviews, first-person observations, and backup written materials.

Consider the journalistic methodology and purposes that Luke says guided him as he introduced his Gospel to "Theophilus," the unidentified "friend of God." Theophilus, who was apparently the first to receive Luke's narrative, may actually have been Luke's publisher, according to some scholars! In the "lead" or prologue to his Gospel, Luke writes:

> Many have undertaken to draw up an account of the things that have been fulfilled among us, just as they were handed down to us by those who from the first were eyewitnesses and servants of the word. Therefore, since I myself have carefully investigated everything from the beginning, it seemed good also to me to write an orderly account for you, most excellent

Theophilus, so that you may know the certainty of the things you have been taught (Luke 1:1-4, NIV).

The resurrection reports may not fall into the special modern-day category of breaking, daily news. But remember: what you see on the front page of your morning newspaper is only one type of journalism.

Perhaps the first daily "newspaper" was the *Acta Diurna* (translated from the Latin as "daily events," or even "newspaper"). This was a current events sheet posted every day by the government in ancient Rome, beginning in the mid-first century B.C. The purpose was to notify the public about important political and cultural happenings.

Since that early time, the understanding of what constitutes journalism has spread far beyond the daily government report sheet. There is evidence that pamphlets and books on current topics have long been part of the field. As we move through subsequent chapters, you will see that, by most tests, the first-century events recorded in the Gospels and other New Testament accounts certainly qualify as a form of journalism. But by today's practices, they would be published in book or pamphlet form.

With the advent of the printing press, the rise of independent newspapers and other publishers, and more recently, the growth of electronic news reporting, we have developed a broad multimedia definition of journalism. Today, journalistic writing includes such categories as newspapers, magazines, newsletters, pamphlets, internet reports and radio and television programs with a news or "magazine" format. Also, there has been a dramatic increase in journalistic books, which may be the closest cousins in our own day to the New Testament Gospels and the Acts of the Apostles.

These books, which focus on current events, movements, or issues, have gained tremendous popularity and circulation in recent years. Environmental and public consumer books, such as Rachel Carson's *Silent Spring* (1962) on the dangers of pesticides, and Ralph Nader's *Unsafe at Any Speed* (1965) on the defects in a model of the Chevrolet Corvair, have had a major impact on public opinion, legislation, and public consciousness.

In the area of public concern about crime, Truman Capote broke new ground in his *In Cold Blood*. There, he explored the personalities of two killers who were responsible for the senseless, random murder of an entire family in the Midwest.

As for cultural movements, Tom Wolfe's "new journalism" reports have set the pace. *The Right Stuff*, for instance, explored the adventures of the first American astronauts, and like many of Wolfe's other works, helped capture the tone of a series of great events and trends of recent times.

Overall, the accounts of the Resurrection in the New Testament seem to fit rather nicely into this journalistic genre—either as stand-alone investigative articles, or as part of a longer, book-length journalistic treatment of the early Christian movement.

Is There Any Real Difference between Newspaper Journalism and a Journalistic Book?

The difference between the journalism in a daily news story and in a long series of investigative articles or a journalistic book is mostly a matter of degree. The methodology—doing interviews, digging for facts, finding relevant documents—is similar in most types of reporting. But the amount of effort and time to do the research and writing can vary greatly, depending on the format the reporter chooses for presenting his or her account.

To get a sense of what it takes to put together a journalistic report, consider the typical newspaper lying around your home. Every edition usually contains "hard," breaking news, which happened yesterday. Typically, the daily news reporter will check in with his city editor in the morning, get his news assignment for the day—which may be a courtroom trial, a community meeting, or a fire—and then gather all he can on that subject before the day's deadline.

The assigned report *must* be written and turned in to the city desk by the deadline. Or, as I was told when I first started working at the New York *Daily News*, "If you miss the deadline, there will be a white space in the paper where your story should be!"

Next to being dead wrong in what you report, the threat of that white space may be the greatest fear of the newspaper reporter.

While a short, one-day turnaround characterizes breaking daily stories, magazine and newspaper features are different. It often requires days, weeks, or even months of legwork, research, and interviewing to produce stories that may involve analyses of cultural trends, in-depth personality profiles, or explorations of complex public issues.

True investigative journalism—such as the work of Bob Woodward and Carl Bernstein on the Watergate stories, which brought down the Nixon administration—demands even more time and effort. In fact, this type of reporting begins to approach the requirements usually associated with the research and writing of the journalistic book.

The books that I have done with prominent doctors on such current topics as cholesterol and medical error are examples of the journalistic book. They have immediate public appeal, and they may even be highlighted in daily newspaper reports or excerpted in magazines. But like the New Testament resurrection narratives, modern-day journalistic books are a far cry from daily newspaper reporting because they may require years of research and writing before they land on any bookstore shelf.

On the other hand, the fact that something is written in a book or even in a magazine or newspaper, doesn't automatically make it authentic "news." Plenty of stories, which may slip into even the best publications, should never have been printed because they aren't really newsworthy.

What about the resurrection events? Are they newsworthy?

To answer, let's take a look at some of the contemporary tests for real news—and see whether the Resurrection and its aftermath qualify as real news that would make it into print today.

The Acid Test of Newsworthiness

To test the newsworthiness of the New Testament accounts of the Resurrection, consider first some standards suggested by a leading authority on the subject—Columbia University's Melvin

Mencher, author of the classic journalism textbook, *News Reporting and Writing*, 5th ed. (Dubuque, Iowa: William C. Brown Publishers, 1991, 57–60).

Mencher says that to qualify as "news," a report must include these two types of content:

- Information about an important interruption or change in the usual or expected unfolding of events; and
- Information people need to make intelligent decisions about their lives.

Certainly, the Resurrection meets both these general tests. But more specifically, Mencher lists seven other factors that may help a reporter identify what is "newsworthy." These include:

1. *Impact.* Reports that have a significant influence on the public.
2. *Timeliness.* Reports on events that have occurred quite recently—because "news value diminishes with time" (p. 58).
3. *Prominence.* Reports that involve famous people or institutions.
4. *Proximity.* Reports that have some close geographical, ethnic, economic, or other "angle" that establishes a close personal connection to the typical reader.
5. *Conflict.* Reports that feature confrontations between individuals, organizations, or institutions. The conflict may also occur inside an individual—such as anguish over a personal tragedy or a personal search for truth or meaning.
6. *Surprise.* Reports that highlight activities, ideas, or people that are especially unusual or strange.
7. *Currency.* Even if an issue or condition has been around for years—such as poverty or child abuse—it may become newsworthy because of a new public interest in the subject.

"As the historian might say, it is an idea whose time has come," Mencher notes (p. 60).

Although only one of these factors may be enough to qualify a story as newsworthy, the happenings related to the Resurrection of Christ seems to measure up rather well to all seven. First, the events clearly had *impact* because of the widespread implications for human salvation and life after death.

Second, the resurrection narratives qualify as newsworthy because they had *prominence*. Among other things, members of the new Christian sect were becoming public figures in the Jewish-Roman world as they were identified, imprisoned, and even martyred. The movement had become so notorious that it was highlighted by the Roman historian Flavius Josephus, in his *Antiquities of the Jews* (A.D. 93–94).

Third, there is *proximity* in the reports because many readers in widely scattered parts of the Roman Empire were encountering evangelists and other members of the new sect. Some—like Demetrius the silversmith (Acts 19:24, 38) and the owners of the Philippian fortune teller (Acts 16:16–24)—saw threats to their business interests and livelihood. Others were either new converts to the sect or friends of converts who wanted to know more about the new faith. In any event, geographically, economically, or personally they had a close connection to the resurrection reports.

Fourth, the accounts recorded *conflict*, as in the clash between Jesus' followers, who believed in the miracle of the Resurrection, and the religious authorities, who resolved to deny and cover up the miracle.

Fifth, they obviously involved *surprise*. The most dramatic, of course, was the reported miraculous raising of Christ from the dead. But beyond that, a major thread in all the narratives is the strange, unexpected appearances of the risen Christ and the confusion, consternation, and ineffable joy that accompanied these encounters.

Sixth, the resurrection accounts are characterized by *currency*. The growth of Christianity beyond the confines of Palestine into the Greek and Roman world caused an ever-expanding public to want to know more about the new movement. The detailed story of the Resurrection was a report whose "time had come."

Finally, these reports even have elements of the difficult test of *timeliness*. To be sure, the New Testament writers sometimes put down their findings long after the original events. But many of the first-century reporters did write well within the time frame established by many contemporary journalistic books. Furthermore, it's likely that the passage of years in no way diminished the news value for readers such as Luke's "Theophilus," who apparently was presented for the first time with some of the details of Christ's life.

Now, let's pause for a moment and see where we stand in our quest for the greatest news story of all time. First, we know that the New Testament accounts of the Resurrection qualify as journalism—probably under the category of the journalistic investigative report, pamphlet, or book. Second, we know that the Resurrection was by almost any contemporary test "newsworthy." In other words, it would be a major lapse in professional responsibility for a legitimate publication or reporter to fail to cover and publish the story.

But could this news story really be the greatest in history—topping such events as the termination of World War II, the first step of a man on the moon, and the disintegration of the Soviet Union?

Or on an even more basic level, is one supreme story even within the realm of possibility, given all the important, history-making turning points that have occurred in the long history of mankind?

The answer to *all* these questions may well be "yes"—and here are some of the reasons why.

The Ultimate Story

From the contemporary reporter's viewpoint, the Resurrection of Christ is a story that, *if true*, has it all:

- violent death and a miraculous return to life—contrary to all known laws of science;
- supreme cruelty and uncommon compassion;
- serious political corruption and cover-up;
- distrust between the sexes;
- personal betrayal and forgiveness;
- paranormal, "beam-me-up" bodily transport through walls, at blinding speeds, and into extradimensional realms—a kind of electrifying movement that goes well beyond any science fiction fantasy;
- angelic appearances, supernatural messages, and a variety of eerie physical phenomena, such as earthquakes, levitation, disappearing acts, and an empty tomb; and

- supreme love that lays the foundation for the ultimate happy ending.

These factors alone would make the Resurrection one of the most important stories a reporter could ever cover. But the account rises to the absolute pinnacle of newsworthiness if it is really true. We have the clincher if, along with the Crucifixion, the Resurrection was indeed the centerpiece of human history—the door to human salvation and to an understanding of God and the divine realm.

Of course, any street-smart editor would begin with a skeptical, "show me" stance toward any of the above suggestions or claims about the Resurrection. He would ask uncomfortable, even abrasive questions about the purported facts, quotations, and news copy handed to him. He would demand that the reporters feeding him information back up their accounts with confirming witnesses, verifiable details, and other ingredients that go into a plausible, authentic story.

In other words, a tough editor would refer immediately to the basic standard that one seasoned, hard-boiled newsman at the New York *Daily News* communicated to me when I first started reporting in Manhattan.

"Above all, you have to get it right," he said. "No matter how color-fully you write and no matter how impressive your sources, if your facts aren't correct, you fail."

It all comes down to the credo still heard around many of the nation's newsrooms—a saying attributed to a founding father of modern journalism, Joseph Pulitzer. He quipped that the first three rules of good reporting are "accuracy, accuracy, accuracy."

In short, even if the resurrection narratives qualify as a legitimate, newsworthy subject for news reporting and as potentially the greatest news story of all time, there is still one additional set of tests that the report must pass: fundamental journalistic principles require that the facts be reliable and accurate.

This leaves us with three final questions that will set the stage for the heart of this book:

- Just how reliable are the details of the "Resurrection Report" when they are examined under the unforgiving light of modern-day journalistic standards?

- Does the handling of sources, quotations, and facts promote confidence in the accuracy of the accounts?
- Should the average reader accept the New Testament accounts at face value—or at least as readily as he or she might accept a story in *The New York Times?*

To answer these questions, it's necessary to subject the entire Resurrection Report to a much more detailed set of journalistic "field tests"—and that is what the rest of this book is all about.

A Journalistic "Field Test" of the Resurrection Report

In the ensuing pages of part 1, I'll first step into the shoes of a tough, demanding editor. The next chapter, chapter 2, will begin our quest for the greatest news story by laying down some basic rules of first-rate reporting—the standards that must be met if the resurrection account is to qualify as a credible piece of reportage.

Then, in chapter 3, we'll consider the qualifications and work of the six "resurrection reporters"—Matthew, Mark, Luke, John, Peter, and Paul. How good is their methodology, and how well do they handle the facts? In short, how closely do they follow the basic rules of topflight reporting?

Finally, in chapter 4, we'll turn the various accounts over to a "rewrite man"—a special type of journalist who is skilled at combining and merging accounts from a variety of different sources. To evaluate the Resurrection Report properly, it will be necessary to see how well the many facts can be reconciled, and how successfully the disparate parts can be melded into a seamless whole.

With this preliminary part of our investigation out of the way, we'll move into part 2, which contains the heart of the Resurrection Report. Chapter 5 will feature the final version of the "resurrection rewrite," the single narrative that pulls together all the facts cited by the six reporters.

Chapters 6 through 11 deal with the classic questions that every complete and superior news story should answer: Who? What? When? Where? How? Why?

More specifically, these chapters will discuss, in this order:

- *What* is the "anatomy of the rewrite"—or the basic facts, rationale and Bible references that underlie the sequence of events in the composite, rewritten Resurrection Report?
- *Who* are the twenty-six named "newsmakers" who participated in the resurrection appearances—and what was their significance?
- *When*—by year, month, day, and hour—did the New Testament events probably occur?
- *Where* was the most likely location for the tomb—and what else do we need to know about the physical sites associated with the resurrection events?
- *How,* in a physical sense, may the Resurrection have occurred—and does the Shroud of Turin have anything to say to us in answering this question? Also, what are the main objections of the skeptics about what happened to Jesus' body, and what are the merits of those objections?
- Finally, *why* was this event so necessary and significant for human history?

Now let's lay down some ground rules for the remainder of our discussion—what I call the "basic rules of first-rate reporting"—which we can use to field test the resurrection accounts.

CHAPTER 2

The Basic Rules of First-Rate Reporting— And How They Apply to the Resurrection

Just how important is it to know whether the resurrection accounts are true or false?

Since the beginning, the veracity of the New Testament reports has been *all*-important, both for nonbelievers who are considering Christianity, and for believers who are struggling to mature in the faith. Mainstream, historic Christianity has always been rooted in an unwavering belief in the actual physical raising of Jesus of Nazareth from the dead. Or as the apostle Paul put it in his first letter to the church at Corinth, "If Christ has not been raised, our preaching is useless and so is your faith" (15:14).

Of course, the faith of most Christians doesn't depend on logical arguments or proofs about the Resurrection. For the large majority, simple belief in the physical resurrection is enough. But many in our skeptical age want more. They seek some solid assurance that the accounts in the New Testament can stand up to the scrutiny of human reason and analysis.

Most scholars who have studied the miracles of the Bible acknowledge that, for the most part, supernatural interruptions of human history cannot be "proved" or "disproved" by any contemporary test or measurement. In other words, either you believe that Elijah's prayers affected the amount of rain . . . or that Elisha raised the Shunamite's son from the dead . . . or that Jesus turned the water into wine at Cana—or you don't.

But many biblical experts agree that the Resurrection of Christ is in a different category. First, the historic Christian faith rises or falls on the truth of the Resurrection. Other miracle reports do not assume such a level of supreme significance.

Second—perhaps because the Resurrection is so important—more evidence is cited by the biblical reporters to attest to the truth of the event. To be sure, we can't take a trip back in time to check them out—to examine the empty tomb, or question eyewitnesses, or touch Jesus' wounds, as John invited Thomas to do (John 20:24–31). Still, the testimony for the Resurrection far outweighs the evidence for other claims of divine intervention in human affairs. In fact, many Christian apologists—those who defend the faith rationally—regard the Resurrection as so supportable by reason that they highlight arguments for its truth as a basic part of their presentations.

Because the Resurrection is so central to the Christian faith, it has been natural for scholars in a variety of fields to try to test it against their highest standards of truth and authenticity. But what are the best criteria to use?

The most obvious and well-known tools for evaluating and explaining the resurrection narratives have come from experts in the ancient biblical languages, theology, history, and related fields of religious studies. But these are only the beginning.

Lawyers have examined the judicial trials of Jesus, and physicians have used their skills to explore such events as the Crucifixion. As we'll see in chapter 10, the tools of the physical sciences, including chemistry, physics, and microbiology, are proving useful to evaluate the controversial Shroud of Turin, which some believe was the burial wrapping for Christ's body in the tomb.

Despite this wide, impressive array of experts who are scrutinizing the Resurrection under their own special "microscopes," the standards of journalism may hold the most promise of all. Specifically, the journalistic nature of the biblical writing and fact gathering suggests that we should apply the rules that guide responsible journalists and their editors in our own day.

What Are the Fundamental Rules for Reporters—And What Can They Reveal about the Resurrection?

What gives a typical reporter or editor the towering confidence it takes to move ahead of the pack, publish a controversial story, and stand by it, regardless of attacks from news competitors, skeptics, and other opponents?

It all goes back to that quip attributed to Joseph Pulitzer: the reporter or editor must know, beyond any reasonable doubt, that the story is *accurate, accurate, accurate.*

To reach this state of sublime inner confidence isn't easy. The facts have to be tested against the most rigorous rules of superior newsgathering.

The following rules are based on prevailing standards followed by working reporters and teachers of journalism, as well as on my own experience as a reporter, writer, and teacher. The driving *raison d'être* behind each of these rules is the Pulitzer Principle in its broadest sense: the achievement of accuracy, reliability, authenticity, and truth. This is the fundamental guiding principle for any good news story, and no less can be demanded of the resurrection reports.

Although I'll describe and illustrate each of the rules only briefly here, they constitute the basis for our entire evaluation of the resurrection accounts.

Rule #1: Check your facts.

Corollary: Use more than one source to back up important facts.

Reporters are inherently skeptical, in part because they know how easy it is for memory to fail or for bias to shade the facts. Consequently, the best journalists will try to check and double-check their facts, especially the most significant ones.

Bob Woodward and Carl Bernstein of *The Washington Post* set this demanding, two-source standard for themselves in their Watergate reports because they knew the stakes were high—the possible downfall of a U.S. president and his administration. We can demand no lower standards of the resurrection reporters—and they seemed to have lived up to this rule.

A case in point: The empty tomb, which is perhaps the most powerful evidence for the Resurrection, is attested to by all four Gospel reporters. Also, Paul, the fifth reporter, presupposes the empty tomb in his accounts in 1 Corinthians 15 of the resurrection appearances and the overriding importance of Christ's physical conquering of death. Finally, the sixth resurrection reporter, Peter—who actually *saw* the empty tomb and is widely regarded as a major source of Mark's Gospel—assumes the fact of the physical resurrection throughout his first epistle (see 1 Pet. 1:3, 21; 3:21).

Rule #2: Tell the Other Side of the Story.

Corollary: Good reporters should include conflicting or opposing sources, and negative as well as positive characteristics of the featured personalities.

To achieve balance and fairness, good reporters try to present all important sides of a story—and that often means including personal flaws, silly mistakes, and criticisms by opponents.

Paradoxically, citing such negative points may actually work to make the story more believable. With the Resurrection, for instance, you might expect a biased, one-sided set of reports because the New Testament writers were followers of the risen Christ and, as such, had a stake in making the story believable. So it can be disarming to read about:

- *The lack of respect the apostles had for the credibility of some of the most important women.*

The eleven apostles (minus Judas) and a number of other male disciples refused to believe reports about the empty tomb from several prominent women who were eyewitnesses—including both the mother of one of the eleven and the wife of Herod's steward. Not only that, they actually regarded the women's story as "nonsense"! (Luke 24:9–11).

- *The shocking skepticism of one of Jesus' top lieutenants.*

Thomas refused to believe in the Resurrection until he was provided with positive proof—the wounds on Jesus' hands and side (John 20:24–31).

- *A puzzling inability to recognize the risen Christ.*

Mary Magdalene looked straight at the risen Jesus, but she didn't recognize him, even though she had seen him many times before and had been healed dramatically by him. (John 20:14–17). Similarly, Cleopas and the other disciple on the road to Emmaus failed to recognize the risen Jesus at first, even though he walked and talked with them for a long time (Luke 24:13–32).

Although at first such reporting might seem to weaken the reliability of the reporting, in fact this balanced approach *strengthens* the story through honesty. Such openness and evenhandedness also help minimize the impact of any religious bias held by the reporter.

Rule #3: Name sources of quotations and facts.
Corollary: Whenever possible, provide attribution and avoid using anonymous sources.

The reason for this rule is that it's too easy for reporters to fudge the facts when they aren't connected to an identifiable source.

In contrast, stating the name of a specific government official, business leader, or physician acts as a kind of insurance policy that the facts or quotes can be verified. If the reporter was wrong, he and his editor will most likely hear about it from the person who was misquoted, and other reporters will have the means to do their own cross-checking for follow-up stories.

But even though contemporary newspapers and magazines may give lip service to the importance of attaching named sources to important facts and quotations, *all* the major secular publications make exceptions, especially if anonymity is the only way to get a big story into print. Among other things, a source may fear the personal or professional consequences of going public.

Woodward and Bernstein's "Deep Throat," the anonymous source who provided many of their leads in the Nixon-Watergate investigations—and who may have been one person or several (or even nonexistent)—is perhaps the most famous example. But to find others, all you have to do is pick up your daily newspaper and look for quotes attributed to "a government source," or "an industry insider," or "an expert who spoke only on condition of anonymity."

It's common practice these days in briefings of reporters for government officials or other knowledgeable sources to speak "on background" or "on deep background." Under these conditions, the reporter is required to report any published material anonymously. (If a reporter agrees to hear something "off the record," the material cannot be used at all.)

The resurrection reports are strikingly different. In modern-day journalistic parlance, the sources often speak "on the record." In other words, the facts, quotations, and other material that come from an eyewitness or other source can be attributed *by name* to that source.

As the resurrection events unfold, the named sources multiply: Mary Magdalene, the "other Mary," Salome, Joanna, Peter, John, Thomas, Cleopas, and so on. For example:

- We are provided with the actual dialogue between Jesus and Mary Magdalene when she mistook him for the gardener (John 20:14–18).
- At least eleven named apostles (the original Twelve minus Judas) saw Jesus' final ascension to heaven—which occurred after he had spent forty days among them following the Resurrection (Acts 1:1–14). Other possible witnesses to this ascension included Mary the mother of Jesus, and Jesus' four brothers—James, Joseph, Simon, and Judas (see Acts 1:14; Matt. 13:55).
- On the shores of the Sea of Galilee, seven disciples—including Simon Peter, Nathanael, Thomas, the two Zebedee brothers (James and John), and two unnamed disciples —met, ate, and conversed on a number of significant matters with the risen Jesus (John 21:1–25). The fact that five of the seven are identified by name, and that one, John, identifies himself as the writer, adds journalistic credibility to the account.

Certainly, there are a number of unidentified characters in the resurrection narratives, such as the "other women" (Luke 24:10), the companion of Cleopas on the road to Emmaus (Luke 24:13, 18), and various unnamed disciples with the eleven apostles (Luke 24:10, 33). But these are consistently linked to sources that are named or readily identifiable.

Rule #4: Keep your prejudices out of the story.

Corollary: Although complete objectivity is impossible, always try to minimize the influence of your own emotions and opinions in your fact gathering, fact selection, and writing.

Working reporters and journalism texts may claim that objectivity—or a presentation of "just the facts," with no distortions from personal feelings, prejudices, or interpretations—is the ultimate goal of good newsgathering and newswriting. But any hope for total or even substantial objectivity is a pipe dream.

I still recall vividly a story on the vicious killing of a social worker in Harlem, which I was covering as Manhattan Criminal Courts bureau chief for the New York *Daily News*. At first, the facts indicated that we were dealing with a straightforward murder case. But then the radical attorney, the late William Kunstler, got into the act.

In a circus atmosphere that he had helped create, Kunstler had defended Abbie Hoffman and the rest of the "Chicago Seven" against charges of disrupting the 1968 Democratic National Convention. True to form, Kunstler also started stirring things up in the Manhattan case. After taking over as lawyer for the defendants, he injected a racially charged tone to the events and polarized the news coverage.

The reporter for *The New York Times*, either consciously or subconsciously, took up the cause of the defendants. Through her use of positive descriptions of the defendants and the selection of facts that favored them, she in effect positioned the *Times* for the defense and against the prosecution.

I didn't see the situation in quite the same way. Despite Kunstler's arguments to the contrary, I *still* regarded the story as a cut-and-dried murder case. As a result, I played my reporting "straight," trying not to favor either the defense or prosecution.

Predictably, Kunstler loved the *Times* coverage, but he was less than pleased with mine. Every morning in the criminal court pressroom, with all the city's news reports spread out in front of him, he would spend several minutes praising the *Times* reporter. Then, he would look silently in my direction, walk over to my desk, pick up the *News* and turn to my story. Still without uttering a word, he would look at my article, glance up at me, and look back at my article.

Finally, after a minute or so of this, Kunstler would mutter, "Uh huh," and head out toward the courtroom.

Of course, the seasoned old radical didn't fool me a bit. He was engaging in a transparent attempt at intimidation, but I wasn't buying. I continued to ignore his posturing and to write what I regarded as a balanced, objective series of stories.

But was I really being objective?

At the time I thought so. But now, in retrospect, I'm inclined to think there is no such thing as a story that is completely devoid of the reporter's beliefs and emotions. Specifically, in covering that trial I automatically looked for bias in anything Kunstler said. That kind of skepticism or cynicism can skew how you play the facts.

First of all, I tended to be extra sensitive about picking up almost any argument or fact from the prosecution that would contradict or act as a counterweight to Kunstler's comments.

Also, I must admit that as I listened to the evidence in the trial, I became increasingly convinced that the defendants were guilty. Of course, *any* reporter who is listening closely to a case and thinking seriously about it is going to develop some opinions. But once you begin to develop a viewpoint, there is no way to keep a completely open mind about the issues.

Finally, in the very act of trying to keep emotion out of the story, I became less sympathetic to the anguish being suffered by the defendants' families—which was a valid part of the entire trial picture.

In the end, this trial and several after it ended in hung juries. So it seems that the members of the juries were as divided in their attitudes as were the *Times* reporter and I. But the underlying lesson I took away from this experience is that bias and editorializing will *always* be present in news reports—for a number of reasons.

First of all, to get to the heart of *why* or *how* reported events took place, it is frequently necessary to analyze and interpret the facts. That necessitates going beyond the surface events and quotations to their deeper meanings and implications. (For more on this point, see Rule #6 below.)

Second, reporters *never* publish all the information they have at their disposal. Instead they have to *select* the facts and quotations they consider most important, interesting, or relevant. Yet in this very process of selection, they must rely, consciously or unconsciously, on their personal sense of priorities and values to enable them to make intelligent choices. In other words, as they select the facts they will use, they become subjective, not objective.

The Gospel reporter John stands squarely in this selective tradition. In the very last verse in his Gospel, he acknowledges openly that he has been selective in his presentation of the resurrection facts: "Jesus did many other things as well. If every one of them were written down, I suppose that even the whole world would not have room for the books that would be written" (John 21:25).

Unfortunately, modern-day journalists are not quite as forthcoming about their omissions. As a result, unsuspecting and uncritical readers may forget that what they see on the page is only part of the real story—a part they are viewing through the reporter's subjective selection process.

Third, reporters make personal judgments in the way they *organize* and *arrange* their facts. An obvious tool for establishing a point of view is the choice and slant of facts that go into the lead, or the first sentence or two in a typical news story. The reporter sets a particular tone and establishes his overall view of the facts in the lead. That basic approach will tend to stay in the uncritical reader's mind throughout the entire piece—with the result that the reporter's opinion and biases become the reader's opinions and biases.

The end of a story, chapter, or book can send an even more telling signal of the journalist's bias or viewpoint. For example, when I want to check a newspaper or magazine feature writer's personal position on the issues he or she is discussing, I'll go straight to the final couple of paragraphs or "kicker." The conclusion will almost always reflect the writer's personal position (or the position of the editor, who may have altered the copy). A final quote, fact, or observation can be one of the most subtle, yet powerful devices in newswriting for fixing a certain value judgment in the reader's mind.

How do the resurrection reporters measure up to these objectivity tests?

On the whole, all four Gospel writers provide a straightforward depiction of the events and facts, with little injection of personal opinion. When the disciples make mistakes (such as refusing to believe the report of the empty tomb by the women), the reporters "tell it like it is," with little or no embellishment. They describe events, include relevant quotations and dialogue, and mention observable reactions with minimal commentary or editorializing.

For example, when Matthew reports that the eleven apostles traveled to Galilee to receive the Great Commission, he uses a direct, almost flat style:

> Then the eleven disciples went to Galilee, to the mountain where Jesus had told them to go. When they saw him, they worshiped him; but some doubted (Matt. 28:16–17).

Clearly, this is a man who is mainly interested in conveying the essential, unadorned facts. He does not communicate his own feelings, and he does not present an entirely positive picture of the response of the disciples. To the contrary, in his selection of the fact that "some doubted," he demonstrates that the impact of this appearance by Jesus fell short of convincing everybody.

What could we have expected from a more biased reporter? He might simply have omitted this observation.

On the other hand, the *selection* and *arrangement* of many of the other facts and quotes by the Gospel writers does reflect their point of view. They want to show that the reason the tomb was empty was that the Resurrection really happened.

Again, take Matthew. He begins his account just after the Crucifixion with an unusual lead, an anecdote that may have come from Nicodemus or one of Jesus' other friends among the Pharisees. It seems that the Pharisees met with Pilate and warned that the disciples might try to steal his body from the tomb.

So Pilate said, "Take a guard. . . . Go, make the tomb as secure as you know how" (Matt. 27:65).

The Pharisees then put a seal on the stone before the tomb and also posted a guard.

After opening the resurrection story this way, Matthew gives a short account of the resurrection events, including a description of how an angel rolled back the stone and frightened the guards so much that "they shook and became like dead men" (Matt. 28:4).

Then, Matthew returns to the issue of the opposition. He notes that the guards at the tomb returned to the chief priests to report what had happened. The priests then met with the "elders" and devised a plan to pay the guards hush money. They were also to spread a false story—that the disciples came during the night and stole Jesus' body as the guards were sleeping (Matt. 28:11–15).

Obviously, it was in the interests of the followers of Jesus to publish this account of the guards and the allegedly false story about the stealing of the body. But a more detached writer would have done the same. This story of a cover-up and a conspiracy would be *news* in any newsroom.

Rule #5: Ask tough questions.

Corollary: Listen to all a source has to say—but then push the discussion deeper, into areas that may have been forgotten or consciously avoided.

Before conducting an interview for a story, a *mediocre* reporter will do a quick check of previous clippings in the "morgue" (the newspaper clipping library) and perhaps throw together a short list of very general, obvious questions. Then, he may ask one or two of these questions and hope all he has to do after that is just listen to the subject talk. If he is attending a press conference, he will typically listen to prepared statements or other "canned" comments, record them correctly, and insert them in the story without further thought.

A *good* reporter will go further: She will spend extra time preparing in advance for the interview. Usually, this means drafting a list of questions after doing more extensive reading in the "morgue." The reporter may also do some preliminary interviews with experts who know something about the person who is to be interviewed.

This extra preparation helps the reporter ask better questions, which will help to "fill in the gaps" in the interviewee's prepared or initial remarks. The reporter's goal is to bring out points that the subject may have considered unimportant, may have forgotten about, or may even have consciously avoided.

A *great* reporter will do all the above, but then ratchet the process up still another step. The top news gatherer will usually check the facts

with independent sources, such as individuals who are known to dis-
agree with the primary source. This reporter may even return for a
second, more extensive interview with the main interviewee. (To be
fair, I must concede that even great reporters, when placed under
tremendous time pressures with a breaking story, may not have time to
prepare adequately.)

It's evident from the detailed, realistic presentation of the facts and
quotes in various resurrection accounts that the New Testament writers
conducted in-depth interviews with the individuals involved. Luke, for
instance, wasn't present when Jesus appeared to Cleopas and the
unnamed disciple on the road to Emmaus. So he had to dig into outside
sources, including eyewitness accounts (Luke 1:2), to come up with the
extensive, authentic-sounding dialogue that Jesus conducted with the
two men.

Also, Luke's careful reporting—and undoubted probing of the
memories of the eyewitnesses—helped him capture the surprise and
excitement of Cleopas and his friend when Jesus revealed his identity
at the end of the conversation and then disappeared from their sight
(24:13–35).

Rule #6: After you have gathered the facts, analyze, interpret, and draw conclusions.

Corollary: Going beneath the surface of the facts is often necessary to answer two of the basic "reporter's questions": *how* and
why the events occurred. (See chapters 10 and 11.)

At first glance, this rule may seem to conflict with Rule #4—keeping your prejudices out of the story and striving toward objectivity. In
fact, however, a good, aggressive reporter must often rely on his skills of
interpretation and analysis to try to answer the important questions
about the story—"how?" and "why?" Although drawing inferences and
making sense out of the facts may put the reporter in some danger of
editorializing, the risk is often necessary for a complete story.

Here are a couple of illustrations that show how the resurrection
reporters observed this rule:

- Matthew explained *how* the religious leaders bribed the guards who were watching over Jesus' tomb. He also told *why* they felt the bribe was necessary: to spread the lie that the disciples stole the body (Matt. 28:11–15). Matthew obviously felt it was essential to set the record straight in order to counter the false story that was still circulating at the time of the writing and publication of his Gospel.

- John, as the writer-reporter, in effect "steps into" the meeting on the shores of the Sea of Galilee. First, John quotes some words of Jesus to Peter:

I tell you the truth, when you were younger you dressed yourself and went where you wanted; but when you are old you will stretch out your hands, and someone else will dress you and lead you where you do not want to go (John 21:18).

John then explains *why* the remark was made: "Jesus said this to indicate the kind of death by which Peter would glorify God" (John 21:19).

Although there are a few such examples of interpretive reporting by the resurrection reporters, they occur infrequently. For the most part, the authors relate the events without comment and let the facts and quotations speak for themselves.

John, for example, instead of taking it on himself to explain the significance of the encounter between the risen Jesus and the doubting Thomas, let a quote from Christ do the job: "Because you have seen me, you have believed; blessed are those who have not seen and yet have believed" (John 20:29).

Rule #7: *Write clearly, simply and logically.*

Corollary: A well-organized story will often be regarded as well written.

Clear and forceful journalistic prose will focus on strong verbs in the active voice, the choice of precise, descriptive nouns, and sparing use of adjectives and adverbs—except where they add to the accuracy and "color" of the report.

Also, a superior report must be well organized. I can still recall with embarrassment some occasions where editors or literary agents have criticized a piece of my writing as "not well written." In almost every case the reason was my failure to take sufficient time to do a good job of outlining and organizing the facts.

Overall, the Gospel accounts meet these tests. They are written in simple, active-voice prose, and they proceed clearly and chronologically. Each starts with some initial event—such as the posting of the guards (Matthew), the movement of the women toward the tomb on Easter morning (Mark and Luke), or Mary Magdalene's discovery of the empty tomb (John). Then, each reporter proceeds to the last recorded resurrection appearance in his particular Gospel.

As the longest and most detailed of the four narratives, John's news story provides a particularly instructive and challenging illustration of the characteristically clear style and organizational structure used by the resurrection reporters (see chapters 20–21). Here are some specific illustations of John's journalistic style and organization:

• The active voice predominates.
Consider John 20:3–5:

"So Peter and the other disciple started for the tomb. Both were running, but the other disciple outran Peter and reached the tomb first. He bent over and looked in at the strips of linen lying there but did not go in." (Most authorities believe the "other disciple" referred to here is the apostle John, who was also author of the Gospel.)

If this description had been written in the passive voice, much of the clarity and power would have disappeared. Suppose, for instance, John had said, "Peter *was outrun* by the other disciple, and the tomb *was reached* first by this other disciple." Obviously, in this case, the active voice is preferable. Of course, sometimes the passive is appropriate, both in communicating the facts and adding some variety to the story. So John says in 20:7b, "The cloth was folded up by itself, separate from the linen." But on balance, *most* verbs in a hard-hitting journalistic piece should be active.

- John employs specific and interesting nouns, and makes sparing but effective use of his adjectives and adverbs.

To get the full impact of the Greek words and phrases, it would be necessary to go back to the original manuscripts. But the English translations provide a close approximation of John's actual style.

Here is a sampling from chapters 20 and 21: "strips of linen lying there" (20:5); "two angels in white" (20:12); "nail marks in his hands" (20:25); "towing the net full of fish, for they were not far from shore, about a hundred yards" (21:8); "[the net] was full of large fish, 153, but even with so many the net was not torn" (21:11).

- John has organized his story clearly and logically.

Here is a simplified outline showing how John put the resurrection story together—an outline that a modern-day feature or book writer might use to arrange the facts before sitting down to write:

John's Outline on the Resurrection

I.   The first arrivals at the tomb (20:1–10)
A. Mary Magdalene
B. Peter and John (the "other disciple")
II. Mary Magdalene's mistake (20:11–18)
A. Her encounter with two angels
B. Her encounter with Jesus, whom she mistakes for the gardener
III. Jesus' appearance to the disciples, with the exception of Thomas (20:19–23)
IV. Jesus' appearance to "doubting Thomas" (20:24–29)
V.   Short transition paragraph, including writer's purpose and methodology (20:30–31)
VI. Jesus' appearance to seven disciples at the Sea of Galilee (21:1–23)
A. The disciples go fishing, encounter Jesus, have breakfast with him (21:1–14)
B. Jesus has important dialogue with Peter (21:15–23)
VII. Conclusion (21:24–25)

Remember: a basic principle of good journalism is that you must organize and outline your story before you write. Otherwise, you will probably end up with a confused presentation, and important points and quotes may be buried or missing. Obviously, John followed this principle closely, and his account shines as a result.

Rule #8: Use specific examples and illustrations.
> *Corollary 1:* Don't allow a general or abstract statement to stand alone: back it up with a quote, anecdote, or verifiable fact.
> *Corollary 2:* Select details that convey the flavor and "sound" of actual happenings.

In their classic little book on writing, *The Elements of Style,* William Strunk Jr. and E. B. White cited this "elemental principle of composition": "Use definite, specific, concrete language. Prefer the specific to the general, the definite to the vague, the concrete to the abstract" (New York: Macmillan Paperbacks, 1962, p. 15).

The same principle applies to journalistic writing. I can't count the number of times I've said to students in writing seminars—or had an editor or reader say to me—"Back it up! Back your statement up!"

The resurrection reporters follow this principle consistently. For example, in Mark's short reference to the Resurrection, he doesn't just stop with an observation that the women who found the stone rolled away were "alarmed." Instead, he goes on to describe the reaction that the angel (or "young man") had to their amazement.

According to Mark, the angel tells the women not to be alarmed, says that Jesus has risen, and directs the women to tell the disciples that the risen Christ will go to Galilee, where he will meet with them. Also, Mark goes into detail about the women's alarm or amazement at this event. He says the astonishment was so profound and laced with fear that at first, the women didn't tell anyone what they had seen (see Mark 16:5–8).

This kind of detail is characteristic of all the resurrection accounts and plays a huge role in making the reports come across as realistic.

Rule #9: Include realistic quotations and dialogue.
   Corollary: Quoted speech should mirror the rhythms and vocabulary of actual speech. Otherwise, quotes will seem "made-up."

It's always dangerous for a reporter to make up or "doctor" a quote because—unless he or she has unusual talent as a novelist—the concocted version will almost always sound phony. It just won't have the ring of truth, often because it will lack the specificity, rhythm, and vocabulary of actual speech.

One of the ways I like to test the authenticity of printed dialogue is to read it aloud. If it's not real, it usually won't sound real. By this test, the quotations and dialogue in the resurrection accounts are real.

Read—and listen—to some of the words in the resurrection stories:

*   *   *

Jesus said to her, "Mary."
She turned toward him and cried out in Aramaic, "Rabboni!" (which means Teacher) (John 20:16).

*   *   *

So the other disciples told him, "We have seen the Lord!" But he said to them, "Unless I see the nail marks in his hands and put my finger where the nails were, and put my hand into his side, I will not believe it" (John 20:25).

*   *   *

"Don't be alarmed," he said. "You are looking for Jesus the Nazarene who was crucified. He has risen! He is not here. See the place where they laid him" (Mark 16:6).

*   *   *

When they had finished eating, Jesus said to Simon Peter, "Simon son of John, do you truly love me more than these?"
"Yes, Lord," he said, "you know that I love you."
Jesus said, "Feed my lambs."
Again Jesus said, "Simon son of John, do you truly love me?"

He answered, "Yes, Lord, you know that I love you."

Jesus said, "Take care of my sheep."

The third time he said to him, "Simon son of John, do you love me?"

Peter was hurt because Jesus asked him the third time, "Do you love me?" He said, "Lord, you know all things; you know that I love you."

Jesus said, "Feed my sheep. I tell you the truth, when you were younger you dressed yourself and went where you wanted; but when you are old you will stretch out your hands, and someone else will dress you and lead you where you do not want to go." Jesus said this to indicate the kind of death by which Peter would glorify God. Then he said to him, "Follow me" (John 21:15-19).

*   *   *

The above interchange, where Jesus in effect *grills* Peter about his love and tests his level of commitment, certainly sounds like real people talking when it is read aloud. Jesus' questions are short and powerful, and Peter's responses are equally succinct and realistic, as he grows increasingly puzzled and even frustrated with his inability to understand what Jesus is "getting at."

The Greek version is even richer, as Jesus in his first two questions uses the verb for the highest moral, divine form of love, *agapao*. Peter responds with another "love verb," *phileo*, which is used to denote warm friendship and brotherly love. But then in his final question—almost as if to test the full range of Peter's love for and commitment to him—Jesus switches to Peter's word, *phileo*. He seems to be asking Peter if his love is complete, ranging from the divine to the human.

This kind of subtlety in Jesus' probing questions and Peter's responses would be hard to make up, even for the most intelligent and perceptive writer. In other words, it is hard to avoid the conclusion that John really was present at this encounter and recorded faithfully what he had heard. (For more on this passage, including observations on the probable use of Aramaic by Jesus and Peter in their actual interchange, see chapter 6, p. 137.)

Rule #10: Write hard-hitting, attention-grabbing leads.
    Corollary: In longer journalistic writing—such as features, investigative reports, and current-events books—inject a new lead every two hundred to one thousand words to keep the reader's attention.

A lead is the introduction to the story or chapter. The lead must identify the most important thing about the story and express it in the most interesting way possible, so that the reader feels that he *must* know what comes next.

Another useful tip I picked up about leads from a seasoned old pro and feature writer at the New York *Daily News*, Kermit Jaediker—a tip that I haven't heard anywhere else—went like this: In a feature or other piece of writing that is longer than a regular news story, don't stop with your first lead. Insert a *second* lead after you've written 200 to 1000 words or so. Then, put in a *third* lead after the next 200 to 1000 words, and so on. This way, you'll pique the reader's interest over and over as you proceed with your story.

This technique is used frequently by good newswriters, and as we'll see, it's also employed on occasion by the resurrection reporters.

Journalists are taught that there are many ways to write a good lead, depending on the nature of the story and the way the writer wants to tell it. Here are a few possibilities:

- *The traditional who-what-when-where-why(how) lead.*

When a daily news reporter is putting together an article on a breaking story, this is one of the most common, and safest, leads. The idea is to answer *who* is the main subject of the story, *what* was the main thing that happened, *when* did it happen, *where* did it happen, and *how* (or *why*) did it happen.

If possible, the reporter tries to cram the answers to all these five questions into the first sentence, which should be compressed to no more than thirty to forty words, and even fewer words if possible. In any event, it should take no more than two short sentences to do the job.

The problem with this "classic" approach is that it can result in perfunctory, uninspired writing. A reporter may succeed in answering all five questions—but may also put the reader to sleep.

On the other hand, *every* story should answer each of these questions at some point, even if all the answers aren't provided in the first sentence or two. Furthermore, newswriters who put off answering the why or how, may end up not putting this information in at all.

- *The dramatic quotation lead.*

Reporters may use this approach if they have a powerful or startling quote that seems to capture the essence of the story. In a book I wrote for Art Linkletter a number of years ago called *Public Speaking for Private People,* we led off the first chapter with a paraphrase of findings in another book: "It surprised many people to read in the best-selling *Book of Lists* that man's chief fear in life is getting up to speak in public. This dire dread rates above death, disease, bankruptcy, and an extra month's extension of a mother-in-law's visit" (p. 3).

- *The question lead.*

This technique can be effective if you can find one question that sums up a burning issue in the minds of many readers.

In writing about the latest findings on prevention of heart disease, for instance, a writer could most likely pull in plenty of readers simply by posing this question: "What is the best way to prevent a heart attack?"

- *The slam-bang action lead.*

If a reporter is fortunate enough to be working on an action-packed story that practically writes itself, the best idea is just to get out of the way and let the facts take over.

One of my collaborations involved the story of Nick Pirovolos, a former gang leader and inmate of the Ohio State Penitentiary who underwent a dramatic Christian conversion experience and launched a ministry to prisoners and ex-cons. The first paragraph of the first chapter reflected his pre-Christian life and state of mind: "I had been on a fast track for a long time. My life was filled with big money, beautiful women, and the bright red blood of anybody who dared to get in my way" (from *Too Mean To Die,* p. 7).

- *The arresting sentence lead.*

Sometimes, a writer may hit upon one strong and, usually, short statement that establishes just the right tone for what is to follow. One of the most effective single-sentence leads I have used came in *Escaping the Coming Retirement Crisis*, a book I coauthored with R. Theodore Benna, inventor of the 401(k) savings plan (Pinion, 1995, p. 11).

The sentence: "A demographic time bomb is ticking."

The point, which we summed up by the end of the second paragraph, was that Social Security and retirement benefits were in big trouble because of the rapid aging of the American population.

Advertisers led with this line in a full-color back-cover ad in *Publisher's Weekly*, the main organ for the publishing industry. Also, many reviewers picked up on the sentence—and I even saw it used (without attribution) in one general interest magazine!

- *The anecdotal lead.*

This approach is used consistently, and with powerful effect, in front-page features in *The Wall Street Journal*. The writer will often devote two or three short paragraphs to telling a short story or anecdote. Then, he or she will provide a direct statement of what the feature is all about—and suddenly the point of the lead anecdote will become crystal clear.

In a *Journal* story entitled "If Only King Solomon Were Here to Settle This Nasty Dispute," the reporter, Daniel Pearl, devotes the first paragraph to an Ethiopian claim for being the home of the Queen of Sheba. The second paragraph focuses on a Yemeni claim. Then Pearl begins the third paragraph this way: "Which version is correct? Maybe neither" (May 2, 1997, p. 1).

The anecdotal technique is also often linked with another type of opening, the "suspense" lead, which is used rather effectively in the resurrection reports.

- *The suspense lead.*

This lead, sometimes also called the "suspended-interest lead" or the "delayed lead," involves teasing the reader at the outset with only part of the story. Then, as he reads on, the narrative unfolds gradually, and only later does the reader learn how the story finally ends.

The resurrection reporters make effective use of this suspense lead technique, sometimes by combining it with one or more of the other types of leads, such as the anecdotal lead.

Matthew begins with a classic suspense lead involving an ominous meeting of Pilate, the chief priests, and other religious leaders who were responsible for Jesus' death (Matt. 27:62ff.). In effect, Matthew's resurrection account might be characterized as primarily a "cover-up" story: The effort of Jesus' enemies to discredit him even after death dominates the lead and a great deal of the "copy" that follows.

In the lead, Jesus' enemies decide to post a guard so the disciples of the "imposter" will not be able to steal his body and claim he has risen from the dead. In other words, the "bad guys" are taking steps to continue their persecution of Jesus, even though he is now deceased.

To a first-time reader of Matthew's account, the situation may seem impossible, and a sad ending inevitable. The feeling might be: "How can any good come out of such an oppressive situation?"

But then, chapter 28 opens with a secondary lead, which also employs a suspense or "suspended-interest" approach. This lead introduces a train of events that includes an encounter with an angel, a triumphant resurrection appearance, and the memorable "Great Commission" quoted at the end of the Gospel (28:16–20).

Along the way, Matthew resolves the issues raised at the conspiratorial meeting described in the main lead. He notes first that the guards, overwhelmed with fear at the sight of the angel, "shook and became as dead men" (v. 4). A little later (vv. 11–15), he devotes a substantial proportion of his resurrection report to unmasking the "cover-up."

Specifically, Matthew says that when the guard reported what had happened at the tomb, the chief priests and elders decided to bribe the soldiers. They instructed them to say that the disciples had stolen Jesus' body while they were asleep, and Matthew notes that this same story was circulating even as he was writing his account.

A good lead, by the way, will not only set the basic theme of the news story, but will also foreshadow later points and facts that are able to expand, elucidate, or perhaps resolve the theme. Following this principle, Matthew introduces his conspiratorial cover-up theme in the lead and then skillfully moves it to a final resolution later in the story.

Mark also uses a kind of suspense lead—but in his case, it's a low-key, straightforward depiction of the arrival at the tomb of three women: Mary Magdalene, Mary the mother of James (one of the twelve apostles), and Salome (mother of James and John, sons of Zebedee).

Apparently, Mark feels that the events he is about to relate speak for themselves and require no hyped-up introduction to get the point across. All the new reader knows at this point is that Jesus has been killed and buried. The women enhance the suspense by puzzling over who will roll the stone away from the tomb for them.

Then, the reader is caught up in an incredible sequence of events. The women look up, see that the stone has already been moved, and also observe an angel and the unconscious guards. Other resurrection events unfold in quick order.

Luke uses a similar, low-voltage suspense lead, with the women arriving at the tomb and finding the stone rolled away (see Luke 24:1ff.). Then, after describing their encounter with an angel, Luke deepens the uncertainty by noting that the eleven apostles and other disciples refuse to believe the women's story, dismissing it as "nonsense."

The uninitiated reader may wonder, "What's going on here? Were these women just making this story up? Or were they hallucinating?"

As if in answer to this question, Luke shifts to a *second* lead in 24:13 by introducing the adventure of Cleopas and another disciple on the road from Jerusalem to Emmaus. According to the context, both of them were apparently among the skeptics who rejected the reports of the women at the tomb.

The two encounter the risen Christ without recognizing him at first, but at the end of the conversation, their eyes are opened to his true identity (v. 31). They rush to the other disciples to tell what they have witnessed and discover that still *another* encounter has occurred, this time with Simon Peter (v. 34).

Now, the original, "nonsensical" report of the women has been confirmed twice. In fact, the "nonsense" is transformed into hard, undeniable fact during a decisive appearance by Jesus to a large gathering of the disciples in Jerusalem (24:36).

Finally, there is the rich, detailed account of John. His introduction involves a strong suspense lead, where Mary Magdalene sees the stone rolled away and then reports to Peter and John her fears that Jesus' enemies have stolen his body (John 20:1ff.).

At this, the first-time reader might become offended or even angry, and ask, "Why can't they at least leave his body alone?"

Even after Peter and John examine the empty tomb, there is still considerable uncertainty about exactly what has happened (20:9). John capitalizes on this suspense with his *second* lead in verses 11–12. Mary Magdalene, crying outside the tomb, is approached first by two angels, and then by the risen Christ—whom she mistakes for the gardener.

A *third* lead occurs in verse 19, where John combines a dramatic event, the fearful cowering of the disciples in a closed room, with a hard-hitting quote from Jesus: "Peace be with you!"

A *fourth* lead appears in verses 24–25, involving the encounter of Jesus with the doubting Thomas. Thomas' famous comments in verse 25 are just right for another strong quotation lead—and there is also an element of suspense because the reader doesn't know whether or how Thomas' unbelief will be handled.

John uses two more effective leads in chapter 21. The first is an anecdotal lead, a fishing expedition that turns into a major resurrection appearance (21:1ff.). The second is a strong quotation lead in verse 15, where Jesus asks Peter the disconcerting question, "Simon son of John, do you truly love me more than these?"

Because these resurrection narratives are so familiar to many of us, we are at a disadvantage in evaluating their true impact. But try sweeping aside your preconceptions and prior knowledge, and imagine that you are reading these reports as you would the front page of today's daily newspaper. If you can capture that fresh mindset, you may find that the resurrection reports provide the best news reading available anywhere—or any time.

Rule #11: Expect your story to be somewhat different from those of other reporters covering the same event.

Corollary 1: Parts of the accounts may be similar or identical if the reporters have access to the same sources.

Corollary 2: But if any two stories are completely the same throughout, look for plagiarism, fact manipulation, or collusion to make-up a fictitious account.

When I was covering fast-moving events on the streets and in the courtrooms of Manhattan, I was sometimes amazed at how different my published stories could be from those by reporters at the *Times* or *Post*. At first, I might wonder if we had been given entirely different assignments. Our leads might be dissimilar, and many of the other reporters' facts might be unfamiliar to me.

But then, as I looked more closely, I would see plenty of similarities, including some identical comments by newsmakers who had been interviewed.

This kind of divergence in stories written about the same events is a common phenomenon when aggressive, independent reporters are at work—for a couple of reasons.

First, no one journalist, no matter how skilled, can tell everything that happens in a confusing, fast-moving situation. Each will automatically select facts based on his or her insights, interests, and biases; consequently, the final stories are bound to be dissimilar.

Second, one good reporter may dig a little deeper in one direction than anyone else, and another good reporter may explore in a quite different direction. In this situation, the results will inevitably be somewhat different, even though each report still represents a facet of the same story.

I still recall the shiver of fear that ran up my spine when one of the reporters I was competing against would come up with a "scoop," or special facts that no one else had. Not only could I expect to be questioned sternly by my editors, but I would also find myself scrambling throughout the day to catch up with the competitor who had gotten a "beat" (exclusive report) on me.

Of course, there are bound to be similarities when reporters are focusing on the same events and relying to some extent on the same sources. An eyewitness who is sure of what she has seen will tend to tell her story the same way, from one interviewer to the next. Also, if there are printed materials—such as a court opinion, press release, or other formal report—the reporters relying on these documents must begin with the text and quote it accurately. Otherwise, they can be accused of inaccuracy, distortion, or sloppiness.

But two reports *cannot* be *exactly* the same or readers and editors will almost certainly raise issues of fraud, collusion, or plagiarism. Imagine, for instance, if you picked up *The Wall Street Journal* and *The New York Times*, two of the nation's most respected newspapers, and discovered identical stories under two different bylines.

The result would trigger a scandal of unprecedented proportions. The questions raised about the reporters can only be imagined:

"Who was the copycat?"

"Are they married?"

"Is this a bad joke?"

With such an event, the opinion that the reading public has of journalists would reach a new low. As for the reporters, they would certainly be called on the carpet by their editors, and if they couldn't come up with a good explanation, they most likely would be fired.

How do the writings of the resurrection reporters fare with this particular rule?

First of all, although there are some similarities among the resurrection accounts, it is clear that even the reports on the same events have been written by different observers. Here are just a few examples:

- All four Gospel writers report that the stone was rolled away from the tomb, but each gives special details. Matthew, for instance, says that an angel rolled away the stone, but the other writers simply report that the women observed that the stone had been moved.

- Both Luke and Paul report that the risen Christ made a separate appearance to Peter, but they refer to the event in somewhat different terms. Luke says that the eleven apostles and some associates informed the two men who had encountered Jesus on the road to Emmaus about the appearance to Simon (Luke 24:34). Paul just says that "he appeared to Peter" (1 Cor. 15:5).

There is an even more subtle variation in these reports—one that turns on the choice of names for Peter.

In referring to Peter, Paul uses the name Cephas (or *Kepha*), a word in Aramaic meaning "rock." Aramaic was the tongue spoken in Palestine in the time of Christ. This, of course, was the special name bestowed upon Simon by Jesus (Matt. 16:18).

(Note: In other contexts, Peter is also referred to by the Greek word for rock, *Petros*, from which we get the English name "Peter".)

In contrast, Luke at this point in his resurrection story identifies Peter by his original Jewish name, "Simon," or *Simoni*.

Is there any special significance in the choice of different names for Peter in these passages?

Probably there is no deep theological significance. Most likely, each writer was in the habit of using a particular name for Peter—just as one person might call my father-in-law "Jack," while another would refer to him as "John." So perhaps Paul was used to calling Peter "Cephas" (see Gal. 1:18, 2:11), while Luke was more comfortable referring to him as "Simon."

But from the standpoint of journalistic analysis, there may be significance in the use of the two different words for the "Rock." For one thing, the variation in names might suggest that even though the reporters are referring to the same event, they are relying on different sources. Or at the least, they have written up their reports independently. If they were playing "copycat," the same name for Simon Peter would probably have been used in both accounts.

A final point on the differences in the resurrection accounts: Bible scholars have often made a big issue over the wholesale copying of one Gospel into another, especially the liberal "lifting" of sections of Mark by both Matthew and Luke.

Consider, for example, the words of Jesus which are identical in Mark 13:17, Matthew 24:19, and Luke 21:23: "How dreadful it will be in those days for pregnant women and nursing mothers!" (NIV). Or in the more poetic King James Version: "Woe to them that are with child, and to them that give suck in those days!"

This word-for-word correlation among the Gospels may indicate that the writers were relying on the same outside source—either a lost written document, or perhaps the memory of those who had listened closely to Jesus' teachings. Another possibility is that two of the Gospel writers (for example, Matthew and Luke) were copying the third (Mark, for example).

I cite this passage on Jesus' words about the pregnant women for one reason: You can find nothing like it in the resurrection reports. Even though there are some similarities in the facts and quotes, there *are far fewer similarities than in other parts of the Gospels, and there are virtually no identical passages or even phrases.*

Why should each of the resurrection accounts be so distinctive? Do their independence and, in many cases, uniqueness have some special significance?

The most obvious response is that the reporters sensed that what they were writing was of supreme importance for the faith. After all, Matthew was already aware of the strong opposition that was building to the reports about the resurrection and the lies that were being spread to the effect that Jesus' body had been stolen by his disciples.

As a result, the reporters must have taken special care in gathering their research materials and expressing themselves on paper. The better they could present their case, the more impregnable the Resurrection would become to outside attack.

Beyond these rather practical, journalistic observations, a Christian observer might argue that God was also aware of the importance of these passages. He knew, as Paul said in 1 Corinthians 15:13–14, that if Christ was not raised, the Christian faith was in vain. He knew, furthermore, that the resurrection passages would become the most examined and attacked of all the Scriptures.

So undoubtedly, the argument might go, a significant part of the divine inspiration of Scripture involved guiding the resurrection reporters in a special way. Such an extra measure of grace would enable them to put together an exceptionally strong set of accounts about the risen Christ, which could weather the intellectual and spiritual storms of the ages.

In any event, some degree of overlap in no way undercuts the credibility of two different accounts. As we have seen above in our discussion of Rule #11, there is nothing wrong with the same set of words being included at different points in each report of an event. In fact, some identical passages may actually reassure us about the accuracy of all. Partial identity between accounts is fine. Red flags would only be raised if most or all of two accounts were exactly the same—and that's not even close to being true with the resurrection narratives.

Rule #12: Accounts by good reporters covering the same story should not be contradictory.

Corollary: If the facts are accurate, a rewrite specialist can merge different reports on the same set of events into one consistent story.

This rule is in some ways the other side of the coin from Rule #11. Even though there should be differences in the stories written by good reporters, there should be no direct contradictions. If there are, you can assume that at least one of the writers is wrong.

Most liberal theologians and Bible scholars assume that there are mistakes throughout the Old and New Testaments, and so the presence of seeming contradictions doesn't bother them. They chalk up the apparent inconsistences to mistakes that any human writer will make, whether in a newspaper or history book.

But most conservative evangelical scholars are not so ready to write off passages of Scripture as mistakes. They make an assumption that the Scriptures are "inerrant"—and that means without error in every respect, including the historical facts that are recorded.

Of course, even some scholars who hold a very high view of scriptural authority may give up on very difficult or apparently contradictory passages. But instead of totally capitulating, they may fall back on a safety net that has roots in the arguments of those who support the inerrancy of Scripture.

Here's the way this line of reasoning goes: Many conservative scholars have taken the quite logical position that the Bible was inerrant in the "autographs," the original manuscripts penned by the New Testament writers. But they note that it is possible that errors may have crept into the text over the centuries as countless copies and translations were made.

So those looking for an "escape hatch" to save the Scriptures from apparent contradictions or mistakes may say, "Sure, there are factual contradictions in our current translations. But there weren't any contradictions in the original manuscripts. And if we ever find those autographs, you'll see that the contradictions disappear!"

As a journalist, when I hear this argument, I immediately think, "Cop-out!"

To their credit, most evangelical scholars seem to reject this intellectual escape hatch. They say that the translations we have are so close to the originals that any mistakes are minimal. Such a position puts the burden on today's Bible students, including both professionally trained scholars and lay people, to roll up their sleeves and work to resolve seeming contradictions, rather than run away from them.

This is similar to the position that a serious editor or rewrite person would take in dealing with varying accounts of the same story that have come in from several reliable newsgatherers. But more on this in part 2, where we hand over the New Testament accounts for a "rewrite."

For now, let's wrap up our discussion of the rules of first-rate reporting by considering one final rule—an unstated thirteenth guideline which many contemporary journalists follow, but which leads to such bizarre results that it really cannot be included in the basic twelve.

One More Strange Rule

There is one final, implicit "rule" that controls most secular reporting, but which doesn't hold sway in the resurrection reports—and really should have no place in legitimate journalism in any era. This rule is based on a profound skepticism about the supernatural, which says, in effect, miracles cannot occur. The rule might be stated this way:

Rule #13: The causes of events—the "how" and "why" of a story—cannot be supernatural.

Corollary: Look for every possible natural or rational explanation for the cause of a mysterious event. If you can't find such an explanation, conclude with something like "the cause remains unknown."

This approach has been common in both historical and journalistic writing at least since the dawn of the Enlightenment, beginning in the Western nations in the eighteenth century. Historians have elected to record events only in terms of three-dimensional space and time, and journalists have followed in lockstep.

Their basic assumption is that the only reality in the universe—and hence the only thing worth reporting and writing about—is what you can see, touch, smell, taste, or hear. They may sometimes take a step toward the twilight zone by reporting on speculative "science," such as the beginning of the universe or the evolution of mankind. But even specialized religion writers on secular publications have traditionally been reluctant to explore the spiritual realm on its own terms.

In other words, there is an unspoken understanding that it is okay to allow an astronomer or astrophysicist to speculate about the Big Bang, or for a physician to cast about for a medical rationale to explain a dramatic, inexplicable healing. But God cannot be given any special credit.

The logical, end result of this antisupernatural bias is that even if a miracle occurs before your very eyes, you are not allowed to mention God or the supernatural as a possible cause. Yet such exclusion of extra-dimensional causation is a relatively recent practice. In fact, many historical works and journalism-related reports written *before* the Enlightenment were peppered with references to the supernatural.

Here are a few cases in point:

- The Greek historian Herodotus, generally regarded as the first Western historian, revealed in the fifth century B.C. in his *History* of the Persians and Greeks that he believed there was divine retribution for evil. Although he focused primarily on the actions and responsibilities of human beings, he also indicated that he thought the gods were behind many human events.

- Thucydides, another great fifth century B.C. Greek historian, noted in his *History of the Peloponnesian War* (translated by Richard Crawley) that the inhabitants of Epidamnus, a city on the Ionic Gulf, were attacked by "barbarians" but couldn't get any of their neighbors to help. So they checked with the oracle at Delphi and "inquired of the god whether they should deliver their city to the Corinthians" to secure protection. Thucydides reported that the answer they got from the "god" was that they should "deliver the city and place themselves under Corinthian protection."

- Augustine wrote the *City of God* in the early fifth century A.D. to counter pagan accusations that Christianity had been responsible for the downfall of Rome. Throughout this work, he emphasized that God gives empires to men and may judge them for their immorality, or show mercy as he wills.

- Gregory of Tours, in his *History of the Franks*, written in the sixth century A.D., went into great detail about the emotional conversion to Christianity of King Clovis. He also reported that the walls of Angouleme miraculously fell down for Clovis because he had "favor" with God.

- William Bradford, the great Puritan leader, wrote *Of Plymouth Plantation* to recount the trials and tribulations of the English Separatists in the late sixteenth and early seventeenth centuries, both in Europe and in Massachusetts. In his report, he didn't hesitate to state his belief that the Lord calmed storms, answered prayers, and helped his followers find corn seed and avoid starvation in the New World.

Such reporting, which prevailed throughout most of history and opens the door to divine intervention in human affairs, is quite consistent with the New Testament approach. Few pre-Enlightenment historians would have shied away from dealing honestly with a reported miraculous raising from the dead, or the post-resurrection appearances of the risen Christ. In contrast, modern-day journalists and historians would feel almost duty-bound to reject this "supernaturalist" approach to reporting events.

The real import of this "strange" Rule #13 is *not* that it promotes a hard-headed, objective, down-to-earth examinination of the facts. Rather, the rule handcuffs many reporters in their research and prevents them from conducting a truly open, honest inquiry. In short, most modern journalists have paradoxically put themselves in a position where they are sure to miss the real story!

You simply can't explore a reported miracle properly if your editor or your journalism guru says: "You can't say the cause of such-and-such was supernatural intervention—even if you determine it was. Instead, you have to skirt the real issue, or ignore it."

Fortunately, the resurrection reporters did not operate under such constraints. They felt free to explore *all* of reality—both the natural world and the supernatural realm. By rejecting Rule #13, they put themselves in a freer position to tell the whole story and not just part of it.

Now, for your easy reference, here is a recap of the reporting rules that we have been discussing. You may want to use this summary as we move through the profiles of the six resurrection reporters in the next chapter and explore the rewritten resurrection account that follows.

A Recap: The Rules of First-Rate Reporting

Rule #1: Check your facts.
    Corollary: Use more than one source to back up important facts.

Rule #2: Tell the other side of the story.
    Corollary: Good reporters should include conflicting or opposing sources, and negative as well as positive characterists of the featured personalities.

Rule #3: Name sources of quotations and facts.
    Corollary: Whenever possible, provide attribution and avoid using anonymous sources.

Rule #4: Keep your prejudices out of the story.

> Corollary: Although complete objectivity is impossible, always try to minimize the influence of your own emotions and opinions in your fact gathering, fact selection, and writing.

Rule #5: Ask tough questions.

> Corollary: Listen to all a source has to say—but then push the discussion deeper, into areas that may have been forgotten or consciously avoided.

Rule #6: After you have gathered the facts, analyze, interpret, and draw conclusions.

> Corollary: Going beneath the surface of the facts is often necessary to answer two of the basic "reporter's questions": *how* and *why* the events occurred (see chapters 11 and 12).

Rule #7: Write clearly, simply, and logically.

> Corollary: A well-organized story will often be regarded as well written.

Rule #8: Use specific examples and illustrations.

> Corollary 1: Don't allow a general or abstract statement to stand alone: back it up with a quote, anecdote, or verifiable fact.
> Corollary 2: Select details that convey the flavor and "sound" of actual happenings.

Rule #9: Include realistic quotations and dialogue.

> Corollary: Quoted speech should mirror the rhythms and vocabulary of actual speech. Otherwise, quotes will seem "made-up."

Rule #10: Write hard-hitting, attention-grabbing leads.

> Corollary: In longer journalistic writing—such as features, investigative reports, and current-events books—inject a new lead every two hundred to one thousand words to keep the reader's attention.

Rule #11: Expect your story to be somewhat different from those by other reporters covering the same event.

Corollary 1: Parts of the accounts may be similar or identical if the reporters have access to the same sources.

Corollary 2: But if any two stories are completely the same throughout, look for plagiarism, fact manipulation, or collusion to a fictitious account.

Rule #12: Accounts by good reporters covering the same story should not be contradictory.

Corollary: If the facts are accurate, a rewrite specialist can merge different reports on the same set of events into one consistent story.

CHAPTER 3

The Six Resurrection Reporters: Who Are They and How Do They Handle the Facts?

When you set out to evaluate a piece of writing, the best place to start is with the writer. I automatically ask a series of questions about the author, such as:

- Who is he?
- Where does she come from?
- Who are his closest friends and associates?
- What are her personal beliefs?
- What are his biases or prejudices?
- What is her educational background or professional training?
- How much experience has he had in dealing with the subject matter he is writing about?
- What can I find out about her previous writing?

The answer to such questions can give me an idea about the writer's expertise and the slant or angle he is likely to take. Also, this kind of investigation puts me in a better position to evaluate his objectivity and fairness.

Unfortunately, however, most journalists—especially daily news reporters—are faceless unknowns. You may see their bylines on a regular basis, but you know nothing about them as individuals who harbor peculiar beliefs and opinions. This means that to evaluate their work, you must focus only on what they write and watch closely for the turn of phrase or selection of fact that may tip off editorializing, prejudice, or other subjectivity.

On the other hand, posing questions about the author works rather well with better-known journalists. For example, when I pick up a non-fiction article or book by Tom Wolfe, I know from his reputation as a practitioner of the subjective "new journalism" style that I'm likely to get a large dose of Wolfe's personality and opinion woven in with the facts. Also, from what I know of their past writings and comments, I would expect a decidedly conservative slant from columnists Robert Novak and Cal Thomas, and rather predictable liberalism from *The New York Times'* Frank Rich and *The Boston Globe's* Ellen Goodman.

The resurrection reporters fit into the category of "better-known journalists" because we know more about them than just their bylines.

So What Do We Know about the Resurrection Reporters?

To be a resurrection reporter by my definition, a person must have made a significant contribution to the gathering and writing of information about the Resurrection of Jesus Christ. According to this standard, there are six men who seem to qualify: Matthew, Mark, Luke, John, Peter and Paul.

The first four, the Gospel writers, are obvious choices because they have put together the most extensive accounts of the remarkable events following the discovery of the empty tomb.

Paul also qualifies as a resurrection reporter, primarily on the basis of his report of specific events mentioned in 1 Corinthians 15. These include the appearances to James, the half brother of Jesus; to Peter; to the original apostles; and to the "more than five hundred of the brothers at the same time, most of whom are still living, though some have fallen asleep" (1 Cor. 15:6).

Note: After his Ascension, Jesus did personally appear to Paul, who was traveling on the road to Damascus (Acts 9; 1 Cor. 15:8). But strictly speaking, this should not be included as a resurrection appearance because by tradition, the resurrection events began with the empty tomb and ended with the Ascension.

As for Peter, he makes only general references to the Resurrection in his first epistle. But still, he looms large as a resurrection reporter because, in the first place, he was an eyewitness to many of the most dramatic resurrection events. Also, according to many scholars, he was a primary source for Mark's Gospel. In other words, Peter was a "ghost" contributor of important facts and observations for Mark.

Before doing a more detailed check on the backgrounds of these six men, we need to consider briefly one more preliminary issue that might concern an editor: the overlap and similarity of material in the first three Gospels.

All You Need to Know about the Synoptics

Matthew, Mark, and Luke are often referred to as the "Synoptic Gospels" because they are organized in a similar way—a feature that makes it easier to analyze and compare them. (According to various dictionary definitions, the word *synoptic* means "displaying or taking the same or a common viewpoint.")

A seasoned journalist who reads through the Synoptics at one sitting will immediately see that all three contain a great deal of common material—and this might cause some concern. As you know from our discussion of Reporting Rule #11 in the previous chapter, some similarity in the accounts of different reporters covering the same event is to be expected.

But with large-scale overlapping, an editor or savvy reader might worry that reporters are colluding on their stories. Or the similarities might indicate that at least one reporter is plagiarizing—that is, copying the material from another source and passing it off as his own without attribution or permission.

Generally speaking, rules and laws against plagiarism today apply to copying the *form of expression* in another's work. They do not prohibit using the ideas or even the facts of another, so long as the facts can be secured from a public or other generally available source.

So how do the Gospel accounts measure up to today's standards of plagiarism?

First, remember our discussion of the resurrection reports in the previous chapter. All of them are remarkably independent. They contain only a few common accounts, and all of those have significant dissimilarities and have clearly been written by different reporters.

But other sections of the first three Gospels are a different matter. As F. F. Bruce and other scholars have noted, the "substance" of 606 of Mark's total 661 verses are in Matthew, and 380 of Mark's verses are in Luke (*The New Testament Documents: Are They Reliable?*, p. 31).

What is a demanding, skeptical editor to make of this? Obviously, collusion or plagiarism is a possibility—yet such a thought has broad, ominous implications. If the reporters did get together and conspire to create one consistent account, or if they borrowed material from one another without permission, such practices would call into question the authenticity of their entire work, including the resurrection reports.

But before we jump to this conclusion, consider these alternative explanations:

- Little is known about the rules for plagiarism in the ancient world, and so we have only sparse authority to evaluate writers who copied other writers.

There is some evidence, among secular poets who were contemporaries of the Gospel reporters, that copying another's work without permission amounted to stealing. The Roman poet Martial, who lived from about A.D. 40 to 102, once charged that another poet who had copied his poems without permission was a "kidnapper" (Latin: *plagiarius*, from which we get our word "plagiarism").

But even if there were ethical objections to plagiarism in those days, laws and regulations against the practice didn't appear in Europe until after the invention of movable type and the printing press in the fifteenth century.

In any case, it may have been acceptable for Roman writers of journalistic or historical material to copy another person's work without attribution. When sources were cited, the reason in many instances was to establish the quoting writer's authority and knowledge of his subject.

- The similar material in the Synoptics may have been in the "public domain"—just as many writings such as government documents are today. In that case, there would have been no requirement to cite sources or worry about violating some sort of first-century "copyright."

Again, we just don't know what the rules or practices were back then, but it is clear that nothing like our common law or statutory rules on copyright existed.

- The three Synoptic Gospel writers may have obtained their common material not from one another, but from a fourth source or set of sources, which we don't have.

This material may have involved one lost written document; several such documents; a precise, widely circulated oral tradition of Gospel stories and Jesus' teachings—or some combination of these sources. (For a possible biblical reference by Paul to such sources, see 2 Timothy 4:13.)

If there was a common outside source or sources, those sources would most likely have been regarded as highly authoritative—indeed, even divinely inspired. In such a situation, it's understandable that all of the Gospel reporters would have felt free to use the material "as is."

- There may have been a formal or informal agreement among the Synoptic Gospel reporters—or between the three of them and a fourth source—that the common material could be used as it was.

Such an arrangement, which today might amount to a binding legal contract, is an established part of our intellectual property law. In other words, if I own certain literary property—such as an interview with an eyewitness—I can sell or give that material to you under almost any terms that we may agree upon.

Would such an agreement necessarily constitute collusion, or some kind of conspiracy to trick the public with a false account?

Certainly not. There could be many legitimate reasons for such an agreement, such as the desire of all three reporters to publish material that they all accepted as true. Indeed, they might believe that varying from or revising the account would be a greater offense than copying verbatim.

So what can we conclude about the common material in the first three Gospels?

There seem to be many good reasons for the material to be there—and a lack of solid evidence of collusion, plagiarism, or the like. So it would be hard, if not impossible, to use the similarities in the Synoptics as grounds to attack the validity of the resurrection narratives.

Now, with these preliminary matters out of the way, let's turn to the six resurrection reporters themselves—and do a bit of "investigative reporting" on their backgrounds.

The Mystery of Matthew

Matthew, the traditional author of the first Gospel, is a shadowy journalist for a number of reasons.

First of all, little information exists about him except what we can gather here and there from a few isolated New Testament passages and snippets of later church tradition.

Second, there is some dispute about whether he and "Levi," the tax collector mentioned in the Gospels, were the same person.

Third, some scholars ask an even more basic question: Was Matthew *really* the author of the first Gospel, including the resurrection accounts—or was some other reporter or writer involved? Also, if Matthew deserves his byline, exactly how did he put the report together?

Let's deal with this third point first.

Overall, the weight of the evidence supports Matthew's right to a byline—especially for the resurrection narratives. Although some dispute Matthew's authorship, the apostle has been identified from the times of the early church as the author of the Gospel that bears his name. Papias, the bishop of Hierapolis in Phyrgia who lived and wrote in the early second century, up to about A.D. 130–140, penned this provocative passage: "Matthew compiled the Logia [i.e., 'oracles' or sayings] in the 'Hebrew' speech [i.e., Aramaic], and every one translated them as best he could." (See F. F. Bruce, *The New Testament Documents: Are They Reliable?*, p. 38.)

The implication is that—despite the overlap of Matthew, Mark, and Luke—Matthew is the sole record of many of Jesus' sayings (Logia), which have been passed down to us as part of the first Gospel. Even more important for our purposes, most of the resurrection narratives in Matthew, as in the other Gospel accounts, are distinctive to his Gospel.

It's impossible to resolve the mystery of Matthew completely from our vantage point, since we are two thousand years removed from the location of his "beat." But the information we have is solid enough for a modern-day editor to feel comfortable putting the following information into his "bio," or biographical sketch:

- Matthew was a Jewish tax collector who worked for Herod Antipas, tetrarch of Galilee. (See Matt. 9:9 for his job description. His most likely boss, given his duties, was Herod. That he was Jewish is suggested not only by his job, but by his name, which means literally "gift of Yahweh.")
- Matthew was sitting in a tax office in Capernaum, on the northeast shore of the Sea of Galilee, when Jesus called out to him, "Follow me" (Matt. 9:9).
- He became one of the twelve apostles—and is mentioned in all

four New Testament lists (Matt. 10:2–4; Mark 3:16–19; Luke 6:14–16; and Acts 1:13).

- Although the Bible never says so explicitly, Levi and Matthew were *almost certainly* one and the same person.

The argument goes like this: First of all, having two names was apparently a common practice in those ancient eastern provinces of the Roman Empire. Here are some cases in point from what we know about the apostles:

—Simon = Peter
—James and John = Boanerges ("Sons of Thunder")
—Thomas = Didymus ("Twin")
—Paul = Saul

Also, there are a number of other very likely double names: Bartholomew was also Nathanael; Judas, son of James, was called Thaddaeus and Lebbaeus, both of which are terms of endearment; and Simon the Zealot was Simon the Cananean.

Clearly, in light of this tradition of multiple personal names, it would have been understandable for Matthew also to have had another name—i.e., "Levi."

Various verses also support this conclusion. For example, it seems evident that Mark and Luke were talking about the same tax collector when they described the feast he gave for Jesus—although Mark and Luke call the host "Levi" (in the NIV) and Matthew calls him "Matthew" (Mark 2:15; Luke 5:29; Matt. 9:10).

If I were writing up a reporter's bio, then, I would come down on the side of those who say that Matthew is Levi.

- Matthew (Levi) *may* have been the brother of one of the other twelve apostles, James the son of Alphaeus (Mark 3:17).

The reason is that Matthew (Levi) was *also* the son of an Alphaeus (Mark 2:14). Because the name Alphaeus may have been used by two different fathers, however, this point remains speculative.

- Matthew *may* have carried the gospel to Persia (modern-day Iran), and to Egypt, where it's *possible* that he was martyred. If any editor included this information, however, he would be ethically bound to introduce it by a qualification like this:

"There are also widespread but unsubstantiated reports" that Matthew did thus and so.

To sum up then, Matthew the man may be something of a mystery. But there is every reason to think that he really is the one who wrote the first Gospel—and its resurrection story. His date of publication certainly lay somewhere in the period A.D. 40 to 100, and various scholars have picked dates from the beginning to the end of that range of years. Probably the finished product came out somewhere between A.D. 50 and 70.

It's likely that he wrote his account in the Syrian city of Antioch, with a largely Jewish audience in mind. His major themes, for instance, include the messianic role of Jesus, the fulfillment of Hebrew Scripture, and Jesus' views on the Mosaic Law.

Matthew's concern about the relationship of the new faith to the Jews of his day carries over into his resurrection accounts. As we have seen in chapter 2, he includes a heavy emphasis on the "cover-up" by the chief priest and religious elders, who feared that the people might really believe Jesus had been raised from the dead.

Mark: A "Spiritual Work in Progress"

Mark, the traditional author of the second Gospel and the second resurrection report, was a "spiritual work in progress" in the sense that we can actually watch him mature and develop throughout the pages of the New Testament.

To pull together his bio, we have to wend our way through a number of isolated verses and passages—almost as though we were on a biblical treasure hunt. But before we start, it's necessary to make one basic assumption: The "Mark" and "John Mark" of the New Testament are the same person. Many modern scholars agree with this position, and the New Testament texts support it.

Now, here are the facts:

Young John Mark, a resident of Jerusalem in the first half of the first century A.D., was the son of a Jewish convert to Christianity, Mary, who made her home available as a meeting place for the early believers. The first possible biblical reference to Mark occurs in Mark 14:51–52:

> A young man, wearing nothing but a linen garment, was following Jesus. When they seized him, he fled naked, leaving his garment behind.

This is an odd passage because, at first glance, it doesn't seem to fit into the narrative. Why would Mark include this seemingly minor detail? Perhaps because the event was actually a major turning point in Mark's life—his first serious, high-risk encounter with Jesus.

The rest of the passages relating to Mark are less speculative. Sometime around A.D. 41–44, just after the execution by Herod Agrippa I of James, brother of John, Herod imprisoned Peter. But according to Luke (Acts 12:12), the church members began to pray, and Peter was released through the miraculous intervention of an angel. At that point, he headed directly to the home of Mary, Mark's mother, where the believers were *still* praying.

Apparently, Mary was a woman of some substance, not only because she had the means to act as hostess, but also because she had at least one servant, a girl named Rhoda, who met Peter at the door (Acts 12:13).

Although Luke, in his account in Acts, is silent on the details, John Mark apparently impressed both Paul and Barnabas enough for them to invite him to join them on their first missionary journey (Acts 12:25). Also, Mark was Barnabas's cousin—a blood relationship that might have given him an inside track for the honor of accompanying the senior missionaries (Col. 4:10).

During his subsequent travels, Mark got involved in a number of adventures. First, he journeyed with the two more experienced missionaries to Antioch in Syria. There, various prophets and teachers prayed and fasted, and the Holy Spirit set apart Barnabas and Saul for their missionary work. Then, the two plus Mark embarked on an evangelistic foray to a number of places, including Cyprus and Perga in Pamphylia, on the southern coast of modern-day Turkey.

During these travels, Mark acted as a "helper" or "assistant" for Paul and Barnabas. The Greek word *huperetes* means literally a "rower" or "member of a ship's crew," and was also used to designate an attendant, perhaps one who handled documents and gave them to others.

Along the way, Mark had rare opportunities to observe and learn how the gospel could be conveyed to the Roman world. For example, Paul and Barnabas brought the gospel to a Roman proconsul and clashed with a Jewish magician and false prophet named Bar-Jesus, who was temporarily blinded by a curse (Acts 13:1–12).

For some reason, all this was apparently too much for Mark, who left the other two at Perga and returned to Jerusalem. This departure displeased Paul, who regarded Mark as a deserter. Paul and Barnabas completed their journey together, but a later disagreement over the "Mark issue" became so sharp that Paul and Barnabas split up. Paul then linked up with Silas for his second and third missionary journeys, and Barnabas took Mark back to Cyprus (Acts 15:36–41).

Fortunately, the story of Paul's relationship with Mark has a happy ending. We learn from Paul's letters that by the time he was imprisoned in Rome, the two had been reconciled, and Mark actually became "helpful" once again to his old boss (see 2 Tim. 4:11; Col. 4:10; Philem. 24).

Even more significant for our purposes, Mark cultivated a relationship with the apostle Peter during these years. In fact, when the two of them were working together in Rome, Peter referred at one point to Mark as "my son Mark" (1 Pet. 5:13). This close personal connection apparently led to what I call the "Peter factor" in Mark—or Mark's role as Peter's voice and even collaborator in the second Gospel.

The Peter Factor in Mark

In our discussion of Matthew's bio, we met Papias, the early second-century bishop of Hierapolis, who lived and wrote in the first part of the second century A.D. The bishop also has recorded an early link between Mark and Peter in the writing of the second Gospel. Quoted by Eusebius of Caesarea, a fourth-century Christian historian, Papias said:

This also the Elder said: Mark, who became Peter's interpreter, wrote accurately, though not in order, all that he remembered of the things said and done by the Lord. For he had neither heard the Lord nor been one of his followers, but afterward, as I said, he had followed Peter, who used to compose his discourses with a view to the needs [of his hearers], but not as if he were composing a systematic account of the Lord's sayings. So Mark did nothing blameworthy in thus writing some things just as he remembered them; for he was careful of this one thing, to omit none of the things he had heard and to state no untruth therein (*The Interpreter's Dictionary of the Bible*, vol. 3, p. 267).

In other words, according to Papias, John Mark spent time "following" Peter, listening to his teachings, and keeping accurate written records. Several other second-century Christian writers and sources have confirmed this relationship, including Justin Martyr, Irenaeus, and the so-called "Anti-Marcionite Prologue" of about A.D. 180.

Why would Peter consent to having Mark do the writing of the Gospel? Probably for some of the same reasons that people today enlist the services of writers.

First of all, he may not have had the time or inclination to sit down and do a lengthy piece of writing.

Second, there is evidence that Peter was not well educated. The elders and scribes in the Sanhedrin, who were the religious rulers of the Jews, regarded him and John as "unschooled" or "unlearned," and "ignorant," according to Acts 4:13. So Peter may have felt inadequate or actually may have been unable to write an acceptable account.

Finally, Peter was in the habit of using other writers. In 1 Peter 5:12, for instance, he says, "With the help of Silas [or Silvanus, according to some translations and the original Greek], whom I regard as a faithful brother, I have written to you briefly."

This special acknowldgment of the role of Silas seems to give him even more credit than might be accorded an amanuensis, or recorder. (But some authorities believe that even an amanuensis in those ancient days might have had significant input in the shaping of a letter or other writing.) In effect, Peter seems to be recognizing Silas almost as a collaborator.

So there are plenty of precedents that would support the idea that Peter might have entered into a collaboration with Mark on the second Gospel. But several questions remain about how they proceeded with their joint project, including the time of Mark's interviews with Peter.

When Did Mark Do His Interviews with Peter?

The exact period when Mark was in contact with Peter is uncertain. But here are a few possibilities for linking them up in a way that might have given Mark sufficient time to gather material for his Gospel:

- An early trek with Peter?

Peter left Jerusalem—and the home of John Mark and his mother—for parts unknown after his miraculous release from prison by the angel (Acts 12:17). It is possible that Mark could have accompanied Peter when he departed.

By most chronologies of the period, some time, perhaps several years, passed between Peter's release (A.D. 41–43) and the beginning of Paul's first missionary journey (probably in A.D. 45–47). Mark, of course, would have had to be back in Jerusalem in time to pack his bags and hit the road with Barnabas and Paul (Saul; Acts 12:25).

- In Jerusalem after the "desertion."

Mark "deserted" Paul and Barnabas, in Paul's words, and returned to Jerusalem when they were only halfway through the first missionary journey. While in Jerusalem this time, Mark most likely was in contact with Peter. As we know from the account of the Council of Jerusalem in Acts 15 (around A.D. 49–51), Peter made appearances and arguments at the council.

- An additional decade to do interviews.

Some time after the "sharp disagreement" between Paul and Barnabas and Mark's trip with Barnabas to Cyprus, Mark began spending more time with Peter. Although there is no biblical evidence for the precise whereabouts of either Mark or Peter during this lengthy period, their contacts would most likely have occurred during the years A.D. 51–60.

In any event, both ended up in Rome at least by the early sixties, and by that time, their relationship was quite close. It's at this time that Peter refers to Mark as "my son" in 1 Peter 5:13—a comment that many scholars would date in the period A.D. 62–64.

What can we conclude from this evidence about the relationship between Peter and Mark?

Sketchy as it is, it's clear that Mark had plenty of opportunities over more than two decades to spend time with Peter, listen to his teaching, and interview him. Not only that, he developed a close personal relationship with Peter.

I have been in a position similar to that of Mark many times, both as a newspaper reporter and as a book collaborator and ghostwriter. As a result of those experiences, I have learned that it's important to take advantage of every moment spent with a busy, important person, because you never know when that person will become unavailable.

When I was a New York *Daily News* reporter, for instance, I typically ran around with poised pen and notebook, jotting down my observations and interviews with such public figures as former New York City mayor Ed Koch (he was a U.S. congressman when I interviewed him); the late Nelson Rockefeller, when he was still governor of New York; the late Manhattan district attorney Frank Hogan; and many others.

After I left the *News* to become a full-time book writer, I had an advantage over Mark in that I was able to switch to tape recorders. But the pressures of interviewing and reporting have remained much the same, as I have had to accommodate my schedule and approach to my subjects.

Some cases in point:

- Mother Teresa of Calcutta was available for an interview only in the town of Ballycastle, on the northern coast of Northern Ireland—where, as it happened, some terrorists had just set off bombs. Because I had no choice if I wanted to talk with Mother Teresa, I flew on a moment's notice across the Atlantic from

New York to meet with her in the chilly Northern Irish convent where she was staying.

- I found myself thrusting a tape recorder in the face of Nancy Reagan in the last few moments of one interview when she was having her hair done in her private dressing area. (During our conversation, Ronald Reagan came in, dropped his contact lenses, and started poking around on the floor around my legs in an effort to find them.)

- Warren Avis, founder of the rent-a-car company—with whom I worked as a ghostwriter on a book about entrepreneurs—put me on a tractor at one point when he was unavailable for interviews, and had me cut the grass on his farmland in Michigan.

I've often thought that Mark was probably running about accommodating himself to Peter in much the same way that I have had to operate.

Was It Really Peter's Gospel?

Because most scholars assume that Mark relied on sources other than Peter, it might be going too far to call the Gospel of Mark "Peter's Gospel." But the tradition behind Peter's contributions is so solid that he should probably be recognized as a "ghost" collaborator for the Gospel of Mark.

The involvement of Peter, a frequent eyewitness to Jesus' ministry and the recognized leader of the twelve apostles, certainly bolsters the authority and sense of immediacy of Mark's account. But there is also another journalistic "angle" suggested by Peter's presence—an argument for pushing back the normally accepted date of Mark's publication.

Pushing Back Mark's Date of Publication

Many scholars believe that Mark wrote the final version of his Gospel, including his resurrection report, in Rome—where we know he spent considerable time, both with Paul and Peter. If this was the case, the finished Gospel was almost certainly published during the period A.D. 60–70.

But as we have seen, Mark also had plenty of chances to work on his Gospel before this. You'll recall, for example, that he and Peter were in Jerusalem at the same time. That would have given him a chance to conduct interviews and maybe even do some writing and circulating of part or all of his manuscript.

Most scholars think Mark's Gospel was written in the late sixties—probably between A.D. 65 and 70. Their assumption is that Mark wrote *after* the death of Peter, which by tradition occurred in about A.D. 64–68, during the persecution of Christians by Nero in Rome. Most authorities agree that the date of Mark had to be before A.D. 70, when Jerusalem fell to Roman troops, because the reporter made no mention of this event in his Gospel.

A common argument for dating Mark's Gospel after the death of Peter is that it is packed with material that is unflattering to Peter, such as details of his three denials of Christ. According to this view, Mark would have hesitated to insert this material *before* Peter's death for fear of alienating him or damaging his reputation. But, the argument goes, Mark would have felt free to be negative about Peter after the apostle's death because Peter's position as a Christian leader and martyr would have been secure.

My experience as a book collaborator suggests just the opposite. Most of those I have worked with as a coauthor or ghostwriter have emphasized the need for truth and honesty and have not hesitated to relate stories about themselves that cast them in a bad light—*if* they felt those stories were important to getting their main message across.

Conversely, I have found that when a person's family members or business colleagues have a right of approval, his story is less likely to get a fair, balanced treatment. In a few cases when I have been involved in writing about someone after the person's death, family members or other close ones typically want to idealize the dead person. If such third parties have the right to approve the manuscript, negative anecdotes or observations may never make it into the book.

In any event, from the New Testament portrayals of Peter, I sense he was a straightforward man who, in general, would have wanted to tell the true story, even if part of the narrative made him look bad. He seemed to have been genuinely remorseful that he had denied Jesus, and it is unlikely he would have wanted to be caught in a lie again.

Peter would also have known that even if he wanted to cover up his major failures, there was no way of escaping publication because his denials of Jesus were well-known in the Christian community. Someone else would have spread his disappointing performance all over the front page, and so he might as well be sure that the story was related accurately.

So for several reasons, Peter seems the type who would have been ready to "take his medicine" with an honest portrayal on the big issues in Mark's manuscript.

On the other hand, there are also some telltale touches on less central issues in Mark's Gospel that may indicate nonessential situations where Peter wanted to keep his name out of print. Here are a couple:

- Mark doesn't mention that Peter tried and failed to walk on water to meet Jesus, who was strolling across the waves on the Sea of Galilee.

Matthew, in contrast, goes into detail about Peter's misadventure, including Jesus' rebuke: "You of little faith . . . why did you doubt?" (see Mark 6:47–52; Matt. 14:24–33).

- Mark omits identifying Peter by name as the follower who cut off the ear of the high priest's servant in the Garden of Gethsemane. Also, he does not describe any reprimand by Jesus to this disciple.

John, on the other hand, names the culprit as Simon Peter. Furthermore, John *and* Matthew report that Jesus rebuked the sword-wielding disciple after the incident (Mark 14:43–52; Matt. 26:47–56; John 18:2–11).

Overall, these and other passages—with Peter "fessing up" to major mistakes, but keeping his name out of transgressions he considered less crucial to the story—would suggest to a journalist that the leader of the apostles was alive and well, and maybe even looking over Mark's shoulder as he wrote. If this was the case, the date of writing and publication would have been earlier than A.D. 64–68—and may have been *much* earlier.

What does early church tradition have to say about whether Peter was alive or dead at the time of Mark's publication?

There is considerable conflict on the issue. For example, the late-second-century bishop of Lyons, Irenaeus, and also the Anti-Marcionite Prologue, declared that Mark wrote his Gospel after the death of Peter. In contrast, the Alexandrian church in Egypt argued that Peter was still alive when Mark wrote.

Finally, some recent controversial discoveries of possible early fragments of Mark by Jose O'Callaghan, a papyrologist (one who studies ancient papyrus manuscripts), suggest the date may be moved back to a point before A.D. 50 (see William Lane, *The Gospel of Mark*, p. 18).

What Does Mark's Date of Publication Mean for His Resurrection Reports?

The implications of a relatively early date for Mark are far-reaching for his resurrection story.

If Mark was not only first to publish a Gospel, but also got into print only twenty years or so after the Resurrection occurred, the news value of his account would have increased significantly. His work would have amounted to a "scoop" in the gentile world—a first-time feature report on relatively recent current events that might be found in the Sunday *New York Times Magazine* in our own day.

That his readership lay in the broader gentile world seems fairly evident. We have already seen that Mark may very well have been writing from Rome, and his text shows that he certainly had in mind an audience outside the narrow confines of Palestine.

For example, when he uses Aramaic terms in his Greek manuscript, he defines those terms for his readers. Obviously, he assumes that his readers would not be familiar with Aramaic, which was the language spoken in Palestine in those days.

One illustration is Jesus' words on the cross: "*Eloi, Eloi, lama sabachthani,*" which he translates, "My God, my God, why have you forsaken me?" (Mark 15:34). At least the last two words are Aramaic, while the two references to *Eloi* may have been Hebrew.

Another example: When Jesus healed a deaf and dumb man, he used the Aramaic command, "*Ephphatha!*" Mark translates the word for his readers: "Be opened!" (Mark 7:34).

In summing up Mark from a journalist's perspective, then, I would conclude that:

1. He collaborated with Peter before Peter's death.
2. He was writing to Gentiles and Jews outside Palestine, many of whom had no knowledge of Aramaic.
3. He probably wrote the final version of his account from Rome, though his interviews with Peter, his other research, and perhaps partial or even complete early drafts of his manuscript may have been finished much earlier.
4. His Gospel conveyed fresh news, presented in a direct, journalistic style. His use of concrete examples, the active voice and short sentences—from the opening verses through the resurrection events—reflect the clear, colorful approach that characterizes the best writing in contemporary magazines or newspaper features.

On a personal plane, Mark may indeed have been a "spiritual work in progress" during his early life. But by the time he wrote his Gospel and delivered his resurrection report, he was a seasoned journalist and literary collaborator of the highest order.

Luke: A True Investigative Reporter

Many serious biblical scholars agree on several features of Luke's life and personality:

- He was definitely a physician. Paul refers to him as "the beloved physician," or as the NIV puts it: "Our dear friend Luke, the doctor" (Col. 4:14). Many of the subsequent early church documents also confirm this fact.
- He was a close companion of Paul through many of the great missionary's travels. For example, see Philemon 24 and 2 Timothy 4:11. Also, the "we" verses in Acts show that Luke, who wrote Acts, was present with Paul on many

occasions. These include Acts 16:10–17, 20:2–15, 21:1–18, and 27:1–28:16.

- He was most likely a Gentile, as evidenced from his writing style and vocabulary.
- Luke was probably from Antioch in Syria, according to early Christian tradition and second-century writings.
- He had access over long periods of time to eyewitness and other sources relating to the life of Jesus—though he probably did not know Jesus personally.

For example, while accompanying Paul during the last stages of his ministry and his imprisonment (about A.D. 58), Luke spent a long time in Jerusalem, Caesarea, and other spots where Jesus and the apostles had conducted their ministry (see Acts 21:17ff.).

- The best estimate is that Luke wrote the Gospel of Luke and the Acts of the Apostles some time during the period from A.D. 60 to 70.

More precisely, the second volume, Acts, was almost certainly finished before A.D. 64, when the persecution of Christians by Nero began in Rome. (The reason: Luke makes no mention of this persecution.) Also, it's obvious that before publishing Acts, Luke would have had to go through the experiences at the end of Acts, including the shipwreck with Paul and the first two years of Paul's imprisonment in Rome. These events most likely happened between A.D. 61 and 63.

But now let's look at the front end of the dating scale. What is the earliest possible date for publication of the *first* volume—the Gospel of Luke?

Obviously, Luke would have needed time to gather his material. If he did a good bit of his research during Paul's imprisonment in Jerusalem and Caesarea, he could have finished with his journalistic legwork by about A.D. 58.

In addition, we know he was in contact with Mark while the two of them were in Rome with Paul (see Col. 4:10, 14; Philem. 24). That connection would have given him ample opportunity to share sources with Mark.

Finally, after completing his research, Luke had to sit down to write—a process that probably took at least several months. So the earliest time for publication of the Gospel would most likely have been between A.D. 62 and 64.

But before we go any further in our investigation of Luke, let's dispose of a fundamental question that was raised briefly in chapter 1—a question that also might be asked of the other Gospel writers: Was Luke a journalist—or was he a historian?

A number of scholars, including the British experts F. F. Bruce and I. Howard Marshall, have identified Luke as a historian, and other scholars have followed their lead—without considering the possibility that his work might really have placed him closer to our current definition of a journalist. So what is the difference between the two—and which job description best fits Luke?

Was Luke a Journalist or Historian?

Much has been written about Luke the *historian*—primarily in praise of him because he followed such high principles of accuracy and objectivity.

But remember, many of the principles of research that apply to good historiography also apply to good journalism. Also, the two disciplines often shade off into one another, so that sometimes it's hard to decide whether a piece of writing is history or journalism.

As not only a practicing journalist, but also a person who has been trained in history in college and law school, I have wrestled many times with exactly how you can tell a historical work from a journalistic work.

My conclusion? There are at least three basic tests that can establish whether a particular writing is history or journalism.

History vs. Journalism: The Time Test

It's best to apply this test by answering a few pointed, yes-or-no questions. Usually, none of these will satisfy the time test all by itself. More often, it will be necessary to answer several or all of these questions to come to a conclusion.

- "Are the events relatively near in time to the date of publication?"

If the answer is "yes," you probably have journalism; if "no," history.

- "Is the written report newsworthy, in the sense that it conveys information about recent events, which was previously unknown to many or most of the readers?"

If the answer is "yes," it's more likely to be journalism; if "no," history.

- "Does the account suggest that some sort of action is required on the part of the reader—or will the reader's likely response be intellectual or cerebral?"

If action, it's journalism; if intellectual, it's history.

Now let's see how Luke's Gospel, including his resurrection story, fares with this three-part test.

Luke and the Time Test. First, let's assume Luke began gathering his material in the late fifties and published his account in the early sixties. In that case, his Gospel would have come out *fairly* close to the time of Jesus' ministry and Resurrection. (I'm assuming a date of A.D. 30 for the Resurrection, which would mean a gap of a little more than thirty years until publication of the Gospel.)

The Acts of the Apostles was written and published at a time much closer to many of the events it describes—probably within only a couple of years from the Acts 27 shipwreck and Paul's imprisonment in Rome.

So what can we conclude? As far as being close in time to the events, Acts is journalism. Luke's Gospel, on the other hand, is on the dividing line between journalism and history.

Now, let's move on to the second question about time—the newsworthiness of the account. Again, Acts passes easily: all the material would be fresh and new to most readers.

As for Luke's Gospel, Luke admits that many have written about Jesus' life before. Also, we know that large sections of Mark are included in Luke in one form or another. But 520 of Luke's 1,149 verses are not found either in Mark or in Matthew. Even more important, almost all of the resurrection accounts in Luke are found only in his Gospel. So we can assume that Luke really was conveying some new and newsworthy information to his readers.

Finally, consider the third time question: Does Luke's Gospel call the reader to action?

Luke tells the recipient of his Gospel, Theophilus, that he is writing the account "so that you may know the certainty of the things you have been taught" (Luke 1:4).

In other words, Luke was not writing merely to entertain the reader or to provide some intellectual stimulation. Instead, he was trying to firm up the reader's faith—a challenge that inevitably calls for a decision or response.

The action-oriented moral teachings of Jesus fill much of the middle part of the narrative. Then, when Luke reaches his resurrection accounts at the end of the Gospel, he reports Jesus' promise that his followers will soon be "clothed with power from on high" (Luke 24:49).

Clearly, the Gospel qualifies here as a form of practical, self-help journalism that "hits them where they are living," as one veteran reporter once said to me. This call to faith-based action through the lives of the apostles and early church leaders continues through Acts as well.

On the whole, then, both Luke's Gospel and Acts measure up quite well to the time test for true journalism. And as we'll see, they do even better when evaluated by the next two tests.

History vs. Journalism: The Research Technique Test

Because we have already examined many of Luke's newsgathering techniques in our discussion of the "rules of first-rate reporting" in the previous chapter, there is no need to rehash those points here. But his high standards do deserve some further explanation.

Look once more at the prologue to his Gospel (Luke 1:1–4), where he makes his rules for reporting quite clear. He says that he had access to "many" previous reports—including, most likely, Mark's Gospel. Also, he was in touch with those who "from the first" were "eyewitnesses" and "servants of the word."

He goes on to say in his preface that he "carefully investigated everything from the beginning" and that he has tried to "write an orderly account." If only every reporter would post these guidelines above his desk and follow them!

Finally, after finishing his resurrection account in Luke 24, Luke evaluates the evidence that he has presented about the Resurrection and comes to this conclusion: "After his [Jesus'] suffering, he showed himself to these men and gave many convincing proofs that he was alive" (Acts 1:3).

Proof of the Resurrection was the ultimate goal of Luke's writing because he knew, as did Paul, that faith would rise or fall on the truth of this event. His methodology, described in Luke 1:1–4, was decisive in helping him establish the accuracy and reliability of the report of the empty tomb and the post-resurrection appearances. The reporting tools he chose also marked him as a new reporter.

Luke's Most Important Reporting Tool. Probably the single most important feature of Luke's reporting technique—and the factor that makes him more a journalist than a historian—is his heavy reliance on the *eyewitness interview*.

Typically, when the historian begins to do his research, there are no living people around to tell him what happened. So he must rely on primary sources, such as letters, documents, and other written material produced in the former time, or on secondary sources—including what other historians have written.

The journalist, in contrast, relies heavily on face-to-face interviews with those who have actually experienced the events. Or as John Brady has said in *The Craft of Interviewing,* "The most valuable and original contributions in journalism today are usually obtained in interviews" (p. 1).

Oriana Fallaci, one of the most accomplished interviewers among contemporary journalists, gained fame both for confronting her interviewees with uncomfortable questions and accusations, and also for inducing them to disclose their innermost thoughts.

One of her best-known interviews was with President Nixon's former secretary of state, Henry Kissinger. When she asked him about the reason for his success, he replied, "I've always acted alone. Americans like that immensely. Americans like the cowboy who leads the wagon train by riding ahead alone on his horse" (*Interview with History,* p. 29).

Nixon was furious, and the press had a field day, making fun of Kissinger as "Henry, the Lone Ranger." Although this interview will certainly turn up again and again in future historical writing, Fallaci was clearly practicing journalism, not history, when she got the quote.

Both the Gospel of Luke and Acts stand in this same tradition of journalism, which is rooted in in-depth eyewitness testimonies and interviews.

So under the research tehnique test—which identifies a journalist as one who uses a special, clearly delineated set of techniques—Luke is a writer who must be placed squarely in the news reporters' camp.

History vs. Journalism: The Interpretation Test

There is one final test that I use to distinguish history from journalism—a test that focuses on the use of interpretation and personal opinion by the writer.

Typically, a good historian who writes interesting accounts of the past will take a strong position on the meaning or significance of events and personalities. This is also true of certain types of journalism, such as the "personal" or "new" journalism practiced by writers like Tom Wolfe.

But breaking news stories or investigative accounts typically focus mainly on what has happened—rather than on some deeper meaning or significance of the events. This sort of "just-the-facts" account is clearly different from history.

The Gospel of Luke and the Acts of the Apostles fit quite well into the non-interpretive, breaking news style. Take Luke's resurrection report, for instance. He relates the events in a smooth but unembellished fashion, mostly just recounting the facts and the dialogue. The focus is on what the eyewitnesses have observed, what they have heard, and what they say they felt (such as being "startled" or "frightened" at the appearance of the risen Christ). Luke doesn't inject his own feelings or interpretations into the account. Rather, he lets the facts, quotes, and eyewitness observations speak for themselves.

So by this third and final test—the interpretation test—Luke must be regarded as a classic, old-fashioned journalist who hasn't joined the interpretive "new journalism" approach. To sum up, then, under all three tests Luke seems to be more a journalist than a historian.

On the other hand, John, the author of the Fourth Gospel, might have felt quite comfortable in the literary (if not theological) company of Tom Wolfe, Truman Capote—and maybe even Norman Mailer, despite his recent attempt to write a book on Jesus. Mailer made more significant forays into interpretive journalism with such books as *The Armies of the Night,* about the peace demonstration in Washington in 1967, and *Miami and the Siege of Chicago,* on the 1968 Republican and Democratic presidential conventions.

In his own way, John became an exponent of personal journalism in the first-century Christian community.

John: The First "New Journalist"

John's Gospel, including his resurrection report, is in a different stylistic category from the writing and reporting in the other Gospels. But before we plunge into an analysis of his personalized approach, it's necessary to get a better idea of the man himself. Here is what we know:

- Although there has been some dispute about the authorship of the Fourth Gospel, the best candidate is John, one of the original twelve apostles and the brother of James (probably his younger brother).
- John was one of Jesus' closest companions, along with James and Peter. These three were the only ones present with Jesus for a number of extremely important events, including the Transfiguration (Luke 9:28–36) and the prayer in the the Garden of Gethsemane (Mark 14:33).
- He was the son of Zebedee, who seems to have been a wealthy fisherman with servants (Mark 1:20), and also the son of Salome, who was one of the witnesses to the Crucifixion and the resurrection appearances (cp. Mark 16:1 and Matt. 27:56).
- John was almost certainly the "disciple whom Jesus loved" (John 21:20 and elsewhere). But he and his brother James are never referred to by name in the Gospel, perhaps because of a genuine desire by John to be humble.

- Like Peter, John lacked the educational background of the religious leaders of his day (Acts 4:13).

This doesn't necessarily mean that he was incapable of writing an account like the Fourth Gospel, but he may have had help. For example, a second-century manuscript, the Muratorian Fragment, says that John was urged by a group of church leaders to write down the Gospel in his own name, and then they would all revise it.

The words in this fragment may find support in this statement at the end of the resurrection narratives (John 21:24): "This is the disciple who testifies to these things and who wrote them down. We know that his testimony is true."

In other words, John wrote at least the first draft, perhaps with the help of an amanuensis or other collaborator. Then, an unnamed group of colleagues—who certainly read the manuscript closely and may also have helped with the editing—attested to the truth of what he had written.

- By strong early tradition, John spent considerable time in Ephesus in his later life. From there, he was exiled to the island of Patmos, off the southwestern coast of Asia Minor, where he wrote the Book of Revelation. He is also credited with writing the three epistles of John in the New Testament.
- A few scholars prefer a relatively early date for John's Gospel— some say before A.D. 70. Their reasoning includes the argument that John doesn't mention the fall of Jerusalem, which occurred in A.D. 70.

The large majority of scholars, however, believe John wrote his Gospel at a late date, probably in the decade of A.D. 90–100. Among other things, they argue that the theology in the Gospel is too "developed" for it to have been written at an early date. Also, they say that the omission of references to the fall of Jerusalem and other important historical events can be explained because their significance might have faded in people's minds in two to three decades.

Personally, I find such arguments to be unconvincing. In the first place, a spiritually astute student of Jesus, such as John, who was at the Savior's elbow at many of the important events in the Gospels, would have had plenty of time to absorb a "developed" theology. A full thirty to forty years would have elapsed between the time of the Resurrection (about A.D. 30) and the Jewish wars and other events leading to the fall of Jerusalem in A.D. 70.

Also, much of John's theology is conveyed in Jesus' own words. All a reader has to do is pick up a "red letter" edition of the New Testament, which presents Jesus' words in red, to see how dominant his direct statements are. There also seems little doubt that John and his sources would have memorized or committed to paper many of these teachings soon after they were communicated.

Finally, it's inconceivable to me that the impact of such a cataclysmic event as the fall of Jerusalem would have "faded" from the memory of a Jew who had spent much of his life in Palestine.

To make such an argument is similar to arguing that Jews who went through the Nazi Holocaust should be able to put the tragic experience out of their minds. Some events are so life-defining that they shape a culture—and can never be forgotten. In current editions of *The New York Times*, which is generally recognized as the "newspaper of record" in our own day, you can still frequently find some reference to the Nazi atrocities.

The fall of Jerusalem must have had a similar impact on the Jews of John's day. It's hard to imagine that this event could have been overlooked by a Jew writing about cosmic issues, such as God's plan of historic development and salvation for mankind.

Consequently, I side with the minority who believes that the Gospel of John was written and published before A.D. 70. Furthermore, because of the reference to Peter's death in John 21:19, the date of John's Gospel was almost certainly after about A.D. 64–68, when strong tradition asserts that Peter was martyred in Rome. So the date for publication would have been between A.D. 64 and 68.

A Closer Look at John's Journalistic Style

Now that we know something about John, what can we say about his style of journalism?

Unlike the other Gospel writers, John feels free to inject his own opinions and theological interpretations into his Gospel. Matthew, Mark, and Luke, for instance, begin their accounts with down-to-earth facts or events.

John, in contrast, leads off with a soaring theological prologue (John 1:1–14), which declares that Christ (the "Word") was God, the agent of creation, and the means of the world's salvation. John finally comes down to earth in verse 14 when he introduces the concept of the Incarnation: "The Word became flesh and made his dwelling among us."

Although an interpretive touch is also evident in John's resurrection narratives, he emphasizes action there more than in many of the preceding sections of his Gospel. He also goes lighter on the theology.

With the resurrection report, his main concerns are the events that occurred beginning with the discovery of the empty tomb, the post-resurrection conversations that took place, and the emotions that Jesus' followers felt as they thought about or encountered their Lord.

The reader can actually *feel* the puzzlement of Peter and John, even though they had discovered the empty tomb; the anguish of Mary over the disappearance of the body of her crucified Savior; and the raw skepticism of Thomas. This is the stuff not of abstract theology, but of the most compelling kind of detailed human-interest story (see John 20:1–29).

But even in these action-paced resurrection narratives, John has no compunction about telling his readers the significance of the events—that is, the "why" of the story he is relating. So he inserts this editorial comment in the middle of his report:

Jesus did many other miraculous signs in the presence of his disciples, which are not recorded in this book. But these are written that you may believe that Jesus is the Christ, the Son of God, and that by believing you may have life in his name (John 20:30–31).

After this, John continues with his concrete, events-oriented resurrection narrative in chapter 21—but again, not without some editorial comment. For example, he explains that Jesus had the "feed-my-sheep" conversation with Peter in 21:19 to show how Peter would die. Also, he jumps into his own narrative in 21:23 to explain away an erroneous rumor that arose about the nature of his own death.

So now, we have explored the personalities and journalistic styles of the first five resurrection reporters: Matthew, Mark, Peter, Luke, and John. The final first-century journalist, Paul, had only a little to say about the Resurrection—but his words constitute an extremely important postscript.

Paul: An Important Postscript

After Jesus, the apostle Paul is the dominant figure in the New Testament. His tenacious, courageous evangelism was decisive in giving the early church a foothold throughout the Roman Empire. Furthermore, his letters laid the groundwork for much of later Christian theology.

Unlike Peter and John, Paul was highly educated, a former student of the great Rabbi Gamaliel, a Pharisee, and an expert in Jewish law and tradition (Acts 22:3–4). After leading persecutions against the early Christians and assisting in the stoning of Stephen, Paul was converted on the road to Damascus and subsequently became an equally ardent advocate of the gospel.

The Resurrection was the central event of the faith for Paul. Or as he put it in 1 Corinthians 15:14, "If Christ has not been raised, our preaching is useless and so is your faith." The facts he has passed down to us on the Resurrection are brief, but absolutely essential. In 1 Corinthians 15:3-8, he reeled off a summary of Christ's appearances, which are apparently listed in chronological order:

- A special resurrection appearance to Peter (Cephas), which confirms Luke's reference in Luke 24:34.
- An appearance to the Twelve, which seems to be a collective term referring to the eleven remaining original apostles chosen by Jesus (Judas was already dead). This correlates with the appearance in Luke 24:36 and John 20:19.

- An appearance to five hundred of the "brothers," most of whom were still alive. Some believe this may be a reference to the meeting in Galilee, where the Great Commission was pronounced (Matt. 28:16–20), and I tend to agree. Certainly, anyone who has visited the spacious hills rising abruptly above the Sea of Galilee, near Jesus' ministry headquarters at Capernaum, knows that there would have been plenty of room for five hundred people to witness an appearance and listen comfortably to an address. The text in Matthew does emphasize that the eleven apostles were present, but the reference to "some" who doubted seems to leave room for a larger group. (For more on this, see the discussion of Event #24 in chapter 6.)

- A special appearance to James, the half brother of Jesus. During Jesus' earthly ministry, James had been an unbeliever (John 7:5). This resurrection appearance to him may have been the event that led to James' conversion—and his later assumption of leadership of the church in Jerusalem (Acts 15).

- Another appearance to the apostles, this time to "all" of them. "All" is most likely just another way of referring to the originally chosen eleven apostles, though some feel this inclusive word may suggest that disciples other than the eleven were present. The occasion was probably the meeting at the time of the Ascension (Acts 1:6–11; Luke 24:50–53).

- Finally, Paul says that Jesus appeared last of all to him—a reference to his experience on the road to Damascus. This was obviously a dramatic and personal encounter with the risen Christ. But because it occurred after the Ascension, I do not include it among the regular resurrection appearances. Paul's personal experiences are another news story.

The Resurrection Reporter Wrap-up

Now, the time has arrived for what an editor might call a "wrap-up" of this discussion of the bios and backgrounds of the resurrection reporters.

There are a few generalizations we can make: All of the reporters display a definite point of view on the subject matter of their reporting, in that they are all followers of the risen Christ. Also, all are advocates, in that they want others to believe.

But there is nothing unusual about such beliefs or attitudes. *Every* reporter, today or in the past, has held some personal belief and opinion that could affect his reporting. A friend of mine who won the Pulitzer Prize for exposing Medicaid fraud was obviously opposed to such fraud. Otherwise, he would not have bothered to spend long weeks working on such a story—nor would his reporting have had the powerful impact that it did.

Clearly, such personal opinions and beliefs don't necessarily translate into unacceptable bias. The real issue is this: Is it possible for the reporter to control his or her opinions so that the facts reported remain untainted?

The most truthful answer is that a reporter can probably *never* completely avoid some bias. The selection of facts and turns of phrase will always reflect something about the newsperson's current emotional state, physical health, or personal view of the events. If you are angry or tired, interested or bored, those feelings will most likely show through in your newsgathering and writing.

But despite the inevitable presence of some bias, the New Testament accounts, and especially the resurrection narratives, seem remarkably free of overt advocacy or editorializing. Certainly, the reporters want to prove their points and convince their readers. But they avoid argument and consistently present their facts in an unadorned, balanced fashion, which sometimes even reflects negatively on themselves or on other believers.

In short, the resurrection reporters seem mostly interested in presenting a true account—because they know, from the evidence of their own eyes, or from the testimony of reliable witnesses, that what they are writing is too important to distort or slant.

"Accuracy, accuracy, accuracy!" Pulitzer cried to reporters of the modern era. He could easily have drawn his inspiration from the six resurrection reporters, who nearly two thousand years before had covered the greatest news story of all time.

CHAPTER 4

A Rewrite Assignment for the "Gospel Gazette"

In the last chapter, we roamed around in different parts of the first- and second-century Roman Empire, exploring the adventures, relationships, and spiritual development of the six resurrection reporters.

Now, the scene shifts to a first-century newsroom. The stories from these six reporters have been filed, and the managing editor has sent them to a "rewrite man," who has been assigned the task of merging and reconciling the various resurrection accounts.

To understand why a rewrite man's (or woman's) services might be helpful for our understanding of the Resurrection, let's take a closer look at how this type of journalist operates.

The Rarefied World of the Rewrite Man

When I first went to work for the New York *Daily News*, the scene at the city desk resembled something out of the classic 1928 play *The Front Page*, by former Chicago newsman Ben Hecht and Charles MacArthur. This play helped fix in the public mind the image of the tough, scrambling, big-city reporter—and that was the image that hit me head-on as I reported for the first time to the legendary Harry Nichols, who was in his last days as the *News* city editor.

In those days, the *News* was still the nation's largest circulation daily newspaper, with millions of readers for both daily and Sunday editions. To maintain that lead in readership, the editors kept steady pressure on the reporters whom I saw rushing in and out of the office. They had to be the first with the best story, or the *Times* or *Post* might get the edge.

But in the eye of this reportorial hurricane, there was an island of comparative peace—what we called the "rewrite bank." There, a small group of elite writers would sit, drink coffee, and crack jokes—at least until the 5:00 P.M. deadline drew near.

These were the "rewrite men"—a misnomer because even in the early 1970s, some of the members of the group were women. What was their job description? They had several duties.

In the first part of the day, when reporters were still out on the streets gathering stories, the rewrite specialists might rework stories from the wire services. Suppose, for instance, the Associated Press (AP), United Press International (UPI), and perhaps Reuters had wired different versions of a disastrous fire to the *News*. In that case, a rewrite man might combine them into one narrative. Or if one of the stories seemed clearly superior to the others, he might "touch it up" or "massage" it, as one colleague of mine used to say.

But the main work of the rewrite man was to have his headphones near at hand, so that he could respond quickly when a street reporter was ready to call in a story. As fast-moving, big-city journalism developed, many reporters found they were expected to do no writing at all. Their job was to excel at newsgathering and organizing their notes logically so they could relate the facts in a clear, step-by-step sequence over the phone to the rewrite man.

The rewrite man would type furiously as he received the information. Periodically, he would fire key questions at the reporter, in case a point was unclear or something appeared to have been left out. Finally, the rewrite man would hang up, put the material into final form for publication, and collapse into a heap just as the deadline passed.

Perhaps the most demanding job faced by the rewrite specialist was to juggle the accounts from several reporters who were covering different facets of the "Big One," the front-page story. With multiple reports feeding in through his phone lines, the pressure on the rewriter increased exponentially as the clock ticked closer to the deadline.

A couple of times when I was acting as rewrite man on such a story, I would have other reporters lined up, either on hold, or waiting by a phone for my call. It's been said that the top rewrite men, who are under this kind of pressure day in and day out over a period of many years, suffer more hypertension and other stress-related health problems than workers in any other profession. From my own limited experience in this area, I can believe it.

Although computers have replaced manual typewriters, rewrite men and women have continued to operate in much the same way for decades. Their skills have saved many stories that would have missed deadlines with a slower hand on the keyboard. Over the years, the stellar rewriters at the *News* were probably more important than any other group for making the paper into not only an accurate recorder of New York City events, but also a top-notch, titillating tabloid.

For example, there was Henry Lee, a scholar, grammarian, and Harvard dropout, who was renowned for being able to pull together a full-length story in about five minutes, just before the deadline struck. Kermit Jaediker was an artist in painting word pictures of city life under the most intense time pressure. Theo Wilson, also a great rewriter, gained her fame as one of the few women to crack the ranks of the nation's premier court reporters. Bill Reel, who later became a columnist for the *News* and after that, for *Newsday,* could be relied on to add just the right human-interest touch to a breaking story.

A couple of the resurrection reporters also seem to have stepped into the rewrite role. Luke, for instance, says in the prologue to his Gospel that he used other written and eyewitness reports and in effect merged them into one rewrite job. Matthew also appears to have used this technique.

But no one in the first century actually pulled together *all* the reports from the six main reporters and merged them into one rewritten account. That is what I am proposing that we do in the following chapter through the "rewrite men" on our hypothetical "Gospel Gazette."

But before we get started, you may legitimately ask, "Why go to the trouble?"

Why Rewrite the Resurrection Reports?

There are several reasons why a rewrite can be very helpful in dealing with such an important part of Scripture as the Resurrection.

Reason #1

First, a rewrite, which by definition will combine all the New Testament accounts, can provide a more complete understanding of the "big picture" than just reading the narratives of each reporter independently. With a unified story, the reader can see much better how the entire jigsaw puzzle of the Resurrection fits together—or falls apart.

Reason #2

Second, a rewrite can help resolve confusing passages or seeming contradictions—or can highlight those points that are beyond reconciliation.

Many scholars, perhaps because of theological or philosophical bias, or just plain laziness, have been quick to see contradictions in the Gospel accounts of the Resurrection. Yet in failing to wrestle, as a seasoned journalist would, with the details of different reports, these scholars have sometimes missed deeper insights.

Take the accounts in Luke 24 and John 20, which refer to the first appearance of Jesus to the apostles, and to Thomas's absence from that meeting. If we assume, as many scholars do, that these passages refer to the same event, it would be easy to dismiss two parts of the reports as posing a hopeless contradiction. These are:

1. Luke's statement that the "Eleven" were in the room just before Jesus appeared (Luke 24:33); and

2. John's statement that Thomas was not there, an absence that would have made the count ten, not eleven (John 20:24).

But a rewrite man, applying a "journalistic hermeneutic," if you will, might very well come to a different conclusion. First, he would observe that, when the two men from the Emmaus road arrived to tell their story, the Eleven, plus "those with them," *were* in the room, just as Luke says. But then he would note that Luke is silent about how much time elapsed after the two men told their story. We know only that the group of apostles and a few others discussed the report of the two men (Luke 24:36).

The rewrite man would begin with the assumption that, until he could be shown otherwise, both Luke and John should be trusted as reporters. If he was unable to question them further (i.e., the situation we are in), he might study the two accounts to see whether they were hopelessly in conflict, or whether there might be some way to reconcile them. His reasoning might go like this:

Perhaps Thomas was present at first but then left the group for some obvious reason—such as another appointment or a call of nature. At first, the rewrite man might reflect that Thomas certainly didn't choose the best time to leave, because shortly after he departed, Jesus appeared to the remaining ten apostles. In that encounter, the risen Christ showed them the marks of the crucifixion on his body and imparted some significant teachings.

But then, the rewrite man might realize that Thomas's departure actually served an important purpose: It set the stage for Jesus' even more memorable appearance a week later to the Ten *and* to Thomas. During that meeting, we witness not only the triumph over Thomas' skepticism, but also a message that reached well beyond the early Christian community, all the way to our own time and culture: "Blessed are those who have not seen and yet have believed" (John 20:29).

In such an instance, a rewrite can go a long way toward clearing up confusion and resolving a seeming contradiction.

Reason #3

Third, a rewrite can be a useful way to explore various principles of biblical interpretation.

Some classic principles of evangelical biblical interpretation, or hermeneutics—which may be enhanced or tested by a good rewrite—include the following:

Inspiration by the Holy Spirit. A basic principle that has existed since the first publication of the original biblical texts is that God is the "author behind the authors" of the Bible. In other words, to put it in journalistic terms, he guided the work of the human writers and had the right of final approval over their work.

This divine authorship is recognized many times in the Bible. (See Exod. 31:18; Deut. 4:13; Hos. 1:1; Joel 1:1; John 20:31; 2 Tim. 3:16–17; 2 Pet. 1:19–21, 3:15–16.)

But how did God actually work with his human writers?

This question has triggered considerable discussion among those who have a high view of scriptural authority. Some would argue for what has been called a "dictation theory"—that the biblical writers just acted as stenographers or human "tape recorders," copying word for word what God whispered in their ears.

But a more common understanding of the inspiration of Scripture among evangelicals is that God worked through specific people, whose individual personalities, styles, and backgrounds are present in each text.

For example, it may have been a quirk of personality (such as Peter's embarrassment or defensiveness on some issues?) that prompted Peter to influence Mark to omit Peter's name as the person who cut off the ear of the high priest's slave (Mark 14:47–50). But apparently God wasn't entirely satisfied with anonymity in this instance—so John put the finger on Peter as the swordsman in his Gospel (John 18:10–11).

In a similar vein, Peter may have encouraged Mark to omit both the reference to his failure to walk on water to meet Jesus on the Sea of Galilee, and Jesus' rebuke that he lacked faith (Mark 6:47–52). Mark's account in this instance wasn't in error; it was just incomplete.

But God obviously wanted the whole story to be told. So Matthew was inspired to describe Peter's inability to stay on top of the water, and to record Jesus' rebuke of Peter for his lack of faith (Matt. 14:24–33).

Divine inspiration, then, allows for peculiarities of personality and even personal weakness—but still ensures that all the essential points will be covered.

The centrality of God's plan of salvation through Christ. The assumption behind this principle of interpretation is that the ultimate purpose of Scripture is to communicate the plan of God to save the world through Christ. Consequently, serious readers of the Bible should be alert to messages in different sections of Scripture about Christ and salvation.

The culmination of this emphasis on "Christology" (theology dealing with Christ) and "soteriology" (theology dealing with salvation) can be found in the resurrection narratives.

The independence and primacy of the text. The essence of this principle is that the biblical text is the best authority for interpreting itself. This means that outside theological or other philosophical preconceptions must be given a back seat to the clear words of the biblical writers.

Here is how this principle might work: Suppose that in studying the Bible, a reader insists on being guided primarily by a particular theological system—whether Calvinist, Dispensationalist, Wesleyan, or even the viewpoint of a favorite Bible teacher. In that case, he will inevitably subordinate the text to extrabiblical preconceptions and biases.

Even more dangerous, his theology will almost always take on a cloak of authority that rises above the level of the Scriptures themselves. In other words, the interpretation will become a kind of "super-scripture." Such a result will destroy any possibility of an independent and objective evaluation of the Bible.

From my observation, this is exactly what has happened in many Christian theological "camps," both conservative and liberal. For whatever reason, many scholars seem to have a theological ax to grind. It may be that they are enamored of their Reformed theology, Wesleyan theology, liberation theology, traditional Catholic theology, or some brand of exotic eschatology. Whatever the reason, they view and interpret the Bible through their own special lenses—with inevitable distortions where the text doesn't quite fit into their particular theological mold.

Interestingly, most journalists, even those who have no religious orientation whatsoever, would not fall into this trap. They may be skeptical about reports of miracles; and when they are looking for causes, the supernatural may not come to mind immediately. But at the same time, journalists are trained to cut through the trappings of human interpretation and bias and root out the facts. Their skepticism and "prove-it-or-I-won't-report-it" stance make them shun strong philosophical preconceptions about life. Such attitudes can help an honest, diligent reporter—or rewrite man—figure out what really happened in passages like the resurrection narratives.

Furthermore, the average reader—or theologian—who approaches the Resurrection in a similarly independent fashion will also be much more likely to grasp the true story.

Unity of the Scripture. The assumption behind this principle of interpretation is rather simple—and consistent with the idea of doing a rewrite on the resurrection narratives. Specifically, a belief in the unity of Scripture means that despite its many parts and styles, the Bible should be regarded as one book, with one overriding set of themes and messages.

If this principle is true, then the accounts from the six resurrection reporters *should* fit together. A rewrite that merges all the accounts will help us determine how this can work.

Infallibility or inerrancy. Simply stated, a belief in the Bible's infallibility or inerrancy—a belief that many contemporary evangelicals affirm—means that because the Bible was inspired by God, it is without error in the autographs, or the original writings.

Of course, we don't have the original writings. But as Professor F. F. Bruce and others have pointed out, we do have thousands of ancient texts and fragments that go back as early as the first part of the second century A.D. Because discoveries of new texts over the years have led to few changes in our modern translations, there is good reason to believe that the Bible on your bookshelf today is quite close to the original writings.

But the reliability of a current Bible text doesn't answer the question, "Is it free of error?"

Some scholars, worried about possible contradictions and mistakes they see in the Scriptures, have chosen what might be called a "limited infallibility" path. That is, they say the Bible is infallible as to theology and doctrine, but not as to history and science.

An influential group of evangelicals has taken sharp issue with this position. These believers in "inerrancy" have chosen that word to distinguish themselves from scholars who see the Bible as only "infallible" as to doctrine.

What might a tough-minded rewrite man say about this dispute?

Most likely, if he were fielding frantic calls from Matthew, Mark, Luke, and John on the Resurrection, he would find himself more or less in the inerrantist camp. In other words, he would accept their reports about events, people, and quotations as accurate—unless he could find clear contradictions or errors in what they were telling him.

The clear meaning of the text. A good rewrite man expects to receive clear, straightforward reports over the phone or in notes from his reporters. Furthermore, when he sits down to write, he will observe the basic rules of grammar, syntax, and usage that will help him communicate effectively with this audience.

Similarly, a reliable, classic interpreter of the Bible will rely on standard grammatical, literary, and historical tools to get at the true meaning of a narrative, like the Resurrection. He will take the text at face value, or for what it purports to be. He will allow the account to speak to him, rather than imposing his own ideas and preconceptions on the text.

To put this another way, both the rewrite man and the biblical scholar will take a "literal" approach to their materials and writings. But this term carries such explosive connotations that we need to go into this issue a little more thoroughly before we leave this topic of how to be a good interpreter.

What Does It Mean to Be "Literal"?

The word *literal* has gotten bad press in recent years from the secular news media. When a reporter or editorial writer wants to pigeonhole a religious figure or group as "fundamentalist," he will sometimes tack on the term "literalist" to describe the approach to sacred religious texts. Once the "literalist" label is affixed, the implication is that the individual or group is uneducated, narrow-minded, and reductionistic.

Yet ironically, a "literal" approach is *exactly* the approach that the editors and reporters on *The New York Times, The Washington Post,* and other influential urban newspapers want their readers to take. They expect their public to accept every word they publish as gospel—and most of their readers do!

I cannot count the number of times that I have heard an otherwise well-educated New Yorker make what he or she obviously thought was an argument-ending point: "The *Times* says it's so," or "You really have to read the *Times* today before we can talk about that."

Also, whenever I would stand in line to vote in a New York City election, it seemed that the majority of people around me were carrying the page of the *Times* that endorsed different candidates. The clear message was that they planned to vote exactly as the *Times* recommended.

The point is this: the usual way to read most generally reliable, authoritative types of writing is the *literal* way. This means taking the passages at face value by holding to the primary meaning of the terms and expressions that are used. "Literal" also means not reading something into the text that is foreign to its purpose or literary genre.

So if the text purports to be poetry—as the Psalms do—a literal approach dictates that it be read as poetry, with an emphasis on the figures of speech, artistic content, and emotional impact. With such writing, the reader must pay particularly close attention to the mode of expression and the moral message conveyed.

Figurative language, such as "the trees of the fields will clap their hands," should be treated as a literary device or image that suggests exceeding joy. But we shouldn't violate the primary literary purpose, such as by searching for ways that trees can grow hands and clap them.

In the Bible, there are many other literary genres—such as letters, prophecy, parables, apocalypse, law, biography, history—and I would also add journalism. Each of these must be read and understood on its own terms, not on the basis of some external bias of the reader.

So if a section of the Bible like the conflict between King David and his son Absalom is presented as history, it should be read as history—not as a metaphor about family life. To violate this principle would be like saying that a *New York Times* story about African refugees shouldn't be treated as a factual event, but rather, exclusively as a symbol of some more general truth about the human condition.

Similarly, the literary genre of the resurrection accounts is clearly either journalism or, perhaps, history. To understand the passages fully, we must read them with the journalistic literary purpose at the forefront of our minds. Of course, there will always be some resistance among both journalists and their readers to using even the most thoughtful literal approach where the Resurrection is concerned. Remember Reporting Rule #13 from chapter 2: "The causes of events—the *how* and *why* of a story—cannot be supernatural."

But if we can quote or use *The New York Times* as though it were Scripture, why not give the *real* Scripture a chance? At the very least, when they read the *Times* every morning, most readers give it the benefit of the doubt. Perhaps we should give at least the same consideration to the Bible, which some believe has an even more ancient and venerable reputation than the *Times*.

So let's assume our rewrite man on the "Gospel Gazette" can cast

Rule #13 aside and rise above his prejudices against the supernatural. What guidelines should he follow for his rewrite?

Guidelines for a Resurrection Rewrite

As he sits down to begin his draft, a good rewrite man would start out with these basic assumptions about the six resurrection reporters who have fed him material:

- They are honest. In other words, they are not trying to fabricate stories or otherwise distort or make up facts.
- They are competent. That is, they know their business well enough not to make any silly mistakes in their newsgathering.
- They have their facts right. In other words, the rewrite man assumes the reports are correct—unless they can be proven wrong.
- Although there will be similarities in their reports because they covered the same general set of events, no two accounts will be the same. On the other hand, if they have made no mistakes, the rewrite man will be able to merge their accounts without any contradictions.

A Journalistic Hermeneutic?

These guidelines, taken with the other principles discussed in this chapter, amount to a kind of "journalistic hermeneutic," or a principle of biblical interpretation based on journalistic standards. In a nutshell, this principle may be stated this way:

The interpreter will assume that the accounts of the six different reporters are accurate and consistent with one another unless and until a clear conflict emerges, or until a stated fact is proven wrong.

Now, with this journalistic hermeneutic in mind, let's put the resurrection reporters' accounts into the hands of our rewrite man and see how he does.

PART 2

A Reporter Investigates the Resurrection

CHAPTER 5

The Resurrection Rewrite

The following newspaper-style rewrite of the New Testament resurrection reports is a paraphrase that merges the material of the six reporters who covered the resurrection events. Some "filler" and transitional material that has been added is based on inferences made from the different reports. This extra material may help explain how various events occurred, and how they may fit logically and consistently together.

Of course, if a "God-inspired" rewrite man had worked on this story in the first century, he would undoubtedly have asked the resurrection reporters questions that would have given us the actual missing facts and literary "bridges." In the absence of such a first-century journalistic specialist, we must settle for our current rewrite man, William Proctor, who takes responsibility for any mistakes—and certainly doesn't claim inerrancy or infallibility for his efforts.

These and other technical features of the rewrite will be discussed in more detail in the following chapter, "The 'What' Question: Anatomy of a Rewrite."

IS THE "KING OF THE JEWS" STILL ALIVE?
A Startling Report of a Resurrection in Judea
By Matthew, Mark, Luke, John, Peter, and Paul
with William Proctor

JERUSALEM. In a truly mind-boggling turn of events, the controversial Jewish teacher and accused revolutionary, Jesus of Nazareth—who was reviled and crucified just outside the walls of Jerusalem on Friday, April 7, A.D. 30—has apparently risen from the dead and appeared to more than five hundred eyewitnesses, according to extensive interviews and research conducted by a team of six investigative reporters.

The sequence of events began with a hasty burial and an alleged cover-up conspiracy involving Roman officials and local religious leaders.

A Hasty Burial

After Jesus was crucified on that Friday, he was buried hurriedly in the late afternoon by two members of the Sanhedrin, the ruling Jewish religious council.

The men, Joseph of Arimathea and Nicodemus, had to work quickly before the arrival of the Sabbath at sundown. Under Jewish religious law, they would not have been permitted to perform burial work after that point. As a result, the preparation of the body for burial was only partially completed.

The tomb, which had never been used before and was located in a garden near the spot where the crucifixion took place, was donated by Joseph, a wealthy follower of Jesus. The other Sanhedrin member, Nicodemus, also a follower of Jesus, supplied one hundred pounds of myrrh and aloes. These spices were stuffed quickly into the shroud, which was used to wrap the dead teacher's body. Finally, the men rolled a huge circular stone in front of the entrance.

As the two men worked, Mary Magdalene and the "other" Mary—who was the mother of the apostle James the Less and his brother, Joses—showed up and took seats opposite the grave. Other women also came to the tomb at about this time.

Then, just before the Sabbath commenced at sundown, the women left to buy and prepare some, but not all, of the spices and ointments that were needed to complete the burial preparations. Finally, after the Sabbath had begun, they rested in obedience to the Jewish law.

The Beginning of a Government Cover-up?

Despite clear evidence of death and burial, Jesus' enemies, the chief priests and certain Pharisees, were still worried about him when Saturday dawned, insiders within the Sanhedrin disclosed. Even though this day was a Sabbath, when strict rules for Jews about traveling and contact with Gentiles were in force, the religious leaders arranged a meeting with Pontius Pilate, the Roman procurator of Judea.

According to these Sanhedrin sources, the religious leaders warned Pilate that when he was still alive, the "deceiver" Jesus had said, "After three days I will rise again."

"So please order his tomb to be secured against any intruders until the third day," the religious authorities urged. "Otherwise, his disciples may steal his body and tell the people that he has been raised from the dead. This last deception could be even worse than his other lies."

Pilate went along with the request, but put the burden on them to carry it out. "You have a guard," he said. "Go and make the tomb as secure as you can."

The religious leaders immediately moved to post an around-the-clock guard and put a seal on the large stone that blocked the entrance to the tomb.

Spices at Sundown

Meanwhile, the executed teacher's followers were planning how to complete the burial procedures. At sundown that same Saturday, which marked the end of the Sabbath, three Jewish women, who had been long-time supporters of Jesus, bought additional spices that they planned to use to finish anointing the body. The women included:

- Mary Magdalene, who was widely reported to have been freed of seven demons by Jesus;
- Another Mary—sometimes called the "other Mary"—who was the mother of James the Less, one of Jesus' twelve top disciples, or "apostles"; and
- Salome, the wife of Zebedee and mother of two of the twelve apostles, James and John.

Sometime just before dawn, Mary Magdalene and Mary, the mother of James the Less, walked over to take a look at the tomb. They moved rather slowly because they were carrying the spices they had bought the night before. On the way, they met Salome, who was also loaded down with spices.

But then, as dawn broke and the tomb, which was still in deep shadows, came into view, a disturbing thought struck the three women: "Who will roll the stone away from the entrance so that we can prepare the body?"

At this point—according to the eyewitness testimony of all three women—an extraordinary series of events began to unfold.

An Earthquake, an Empty Tomb—and Total Terror

First, an earthquake struck the area, and the women were so disconcerted that they temporarily looked down and lost sight of the tomb. But when they looked up again, they saw that the large stone had been rolled away during the earthquake.

Leaving her two companions, Mary Magdalene rushed away to tell Simon Peter and the apostle John what she perceived to be the bad news. Apparently thinking that the religious leaders or guards had removed the body, she was distraught when she found Peter and John.

"They have taken the Lord out of the tomb, and we don't know where they have put him!" she cried.

Then, she sought out the other apostles to tell them what she had seen.

Meanwhile, Salome and the "other" Mary, who had remained in the vicinity of the gravesite, moved closer to the tomb entrance. They soon noticed that the guards posted by the religious leaders were lying on the ground, some shaking uncontrollably, others as rigid as dead men.

As they started to enter the tomb, the women saw what had apparently triggered the guards' fright: A fearsome angelic figure in the form of a young man was sitting on the large stone at the entrance, with clothing as white as snow and an overall appearance that they could only describe as "like lightning."

Conversations with an Angel—And the First Eyewitness Resurrection Report

The angel made it clear to Salome and the "other" Mary that the earthquake had accompanied his arrival and that he was responsible for moving the stone. They were utterly amazed and astonished—and afraid as well.

But the angel took pains to calm them.

"Don't be alarmed," he said. "I know you are looking for Jesus, who was crucified. He is not here—he has risen, just as he said. Look at the place where they laid his body. Then go quickly and tell his disciples and Peter this: 'He has risen from the dead and is going ahead of you into Galilee. There you will see him, just as he told you.' Now, I have told you."

At that, Salome and the "other" Mary left the tomb with the intention of finding the disciples to tell what they had seen. But their morning adventures weren't over yet.

According to the women's eyewitness report, Jesus himself met them as they were en route to the disciples and said simply, "Greetings!"

They gathered about him, held on to his feet and worshiped him. Then he reemphasized the angel's message: "Don't be afraid," he said. "Go and tell my brothers to go to Galilee. They will see me there."

The Cover-up Consummated

Sources at the Sanhedrin have disclosed that after the three women had left the tomb, the guards came to their senses and ran back to report to the chief priests all that had happened.

The chief priests and elders then devised a cover-up plan. They bribed the soldiers with a large sum of money and instructed them this way:

"You are to say, 'His disciples came during the night and stole him away while we were asleep.' If this report gets to the governor, we will satisfy him and keep you out of trouble."

The soldiers took the money and did as they were told, according to the Sanhedrin sources. It is also general public knowledge in Judea that this very story is still being widely circulated in that province of the Roman Empire.

A Second Angel

As Salome and the "other" Mary proceeded on their way to the disciples—whom Mary Magdalene was already in the process of contacting—still another group of women arrived at the tomb with spices. These included Joanna, the wife of Herod's steward Chuza. Like the other women before them, this new group found the stone rolled away, but the stunned guards were gone by this time.

Joanna and her companions walked directly into the tomb and saw that Jesus' body was gone, according to their eyewitness report. While they were standing in the tomb wondering about this, two men in clothing that gleamed like lightning suddenly stood beside them.

The women were so frightened and overwhelmed that they bowed down with their faces to the ground.

But the two men said, "Why do you look for the living among the dead? He is not here. He has risen! Remember how he told you while he was still with you in Galilee: 'The Son of Man must be delivered into the hands of sinful men, be crucified and on the third day be raised again.'"

Then, the women remembered Jesus' words during his teaching ministry while he was still alive—and they rushed off to report what they had observed to the disciples.

Skepticism and an Investigation

In waves, the various women—Mary Magdalene; then Salome and the "other" Mary; and finally Joanna and her group—found the eleven apostles and other disciples and told their stories. But the men didn't believe the reports because, as they said, the women's words seemed to them to be "nonsense."

Peter and John, however, decided to investigate further. They both ran toward the tomb, but John says that he was faster and arrived first. He bent over, looked into the tomb, and saw linen burial wrappings—but he didn't enter.

Peter finally made it to the tomb, but he didn't linger at the entrance; he went directly inside, according to John's eyewitness report. There, he saw not only the linen wrappings that John had seen, but also a napkin or towel that had been on Jesus' head. This napkin had been rolled up and placed apart from the linen wrappings.

John says that he then followed Peter into the tomb and, like Peter, saw with his own eyes the linen wrappings as well as the separately wrapped-up head towel. As a result, unlike the other apostles and disciples, John was led to believe at least this much: that what the women had reported about the empty tomb was true.

Peter's opinions after this experience are not a matter of public record. But interviews with John have revealed that neither John nor Peter had a complete understanding of the resurrection at this point because neither was knowledgeable about the scriptural passages supporting the idea that the Messiah must rise from the dead. These two apostles—who with James, the brother of John, were Jesus' closest companions during his preaching and teaching ministry—then returned home.

Mary Magdalene's Emotional Roller Coaster

Mary Magdalene, who had followed Peter and John back to the tomb, lingered just outside the entrance after they had gone home. As she stood there, she began to cry. Still weeping, she bent over to get her first look inside the tomb—and an amazing sight awaited her.

According to her report, two angels in white were sitting on the slab where Jesus' body had been laid, one at the head and the other at the foot.

"Woman, why are you crying?" they asked her.

"They have taken my Lord away," she replied, still under the impression that Jesus' body had been stolen. "And I don't know where they have put him."

Before the angels could answer, Mary Magdalene turned around and saw a man, whom she thought was the gardener, standing behind her. Because her eyes were filled with tears, and also because she wasn't looking directly at him, she couldn't see him clearly.

"Woman, why are you crying?" the man said. "Who is it that you are looking for?"

"Sir, if you have carried him away, tell me where you have put him, and I will get him," Mary replied.

"Mary," the man said—and immediately Mary turned toward him and recognized him as Jesus.

"Rabboni!" she cried out in Aramaic, using a title that means "teacher."

"Do not hold on to me because I have not yet ascended to the Father," Jesus cautioned. "Instead, go to my brothers and tell them, 'I am ascending to my Father and your Father, to my God and your God.'"

So Mary Magdalene took *another* report on her experiences at the empty tomb back to the disciples. This time, however, she opened with a more upbeat message:

"I have seen the Lord!"

Then she proceeded to tell them about her encounter with the risen Jesus, including what he had said to her.

A Secret Rendezvous

Later in the day on that first Easter, Jesus made a special appearance to Peter, according to Peter himself. Because this was a highly confidential meeting, no details are available.

But knowledgeable authorities on the resurrection events have suggested that this special, private appearance may reflect a recognition of Peter's stature as leader of the twelve apostles. Also, Jesus may have felt there was a need to reaffirm Peter and make it clear that he was forgiven despite his denials at the trial of Jesus.

Finally, Peter may have needed some special instructions and encouragement because he was slated to play a decisive role in leading the early Christian community after Jesus' final departure from earth.

The Emmaus Road Incident

On that same Sunday afternoon, two followers of Jesus, who were walking toward Emmaus, a village about seven miles from Jerusalem, reported another highly unusual incident.

The men—one Cleopas and an unidentified companion—were deep in conversation about the reports of an empty tomb when a stranger walking along the same road moved over and joined them. Cleopas recalled the conversation this way:

"What are you talking about on your walk?" the man asked.

"Are you the only person visiting Jerusalem who doesn't know the things that have happened around here in the last few days?" Cleopas replied.

"What things?" the stranger asked.

"Things about Jesus of Nazareth," Cleopas and his companion said, both contributing now to the conversation with the third man. "He was a prophet of God who was powerful in word and deed. Any of the people could tell you that. The chief priests and our rulers handed him over for a judgment of death, and they crucified him.

"As for us, we were hoping that Jesus was the one who would redeem Israel—even though it's now the third day since his crucifixion," they continued. "But some women from our group amazed us just a few hours ago. They came and told us they had gone to the tomb early this morning but didn't find his body. Instead, they said they saw a vision of angels, who said he was alive.

"Then some of our men went to the tomb to check out the story. They found everything exactly as the women had said, but they did not see Jesus."

The stranger heard them out, but then responded unexpectedly with a rebuke: "How foolish you are and slow in your hearts to believe all that the prophets have spoken! Wasn't it *necessary* for the Messiah to suffer these things and then enter his glory?"

With that, the stranger proceeded to explain to them how the Scriptures, beginning with Moses and all the prophets, had actually foreshadowed Jesus as the Messiah.

As the three men approached the village of Emmaus, the stranger indicated in a polite way that he would continue on. But Cleopas and his companion insisted that he stop, saying, "Stay with us because it will be dark soon."

So the stranger joined them in the house where they were staying. As they prepared to eat, the stranger reclined at the table, took a loaf of bread, and blessed it. Then he broke it and began to hand pieces to them.

At this moment, somehow, in some inexplicable way as the loaf was being broken, their "eyes were opened up," as they put it, and they recognized that the stranger was really Jesus. Then he vanished or "became invisible"—again in some way that defied their rational explanation.

Cleopas and his friend stayed in the house for several minutes, reflecting on the incident and trying to absorb its meaning. One observation they both made: "Weren't our hearts burning within us as he spoke to us on the road and opened up the scriptures to us?"

Realizing the potential significance of their encounter with the risen Christ, the two men decided they had to return to Jerusalem immediately to tell the other disciples. So despite the waning daylight, they headed back toward Jerusalem within the hour.

A Meeting with a "Ghost"

When Cleopas and his companion arrived in Jerusalem, they went straight to a house where the eleven apostles and some other followers of Jesus were holding a closed meeting. The doors had been locked because the disciples were afraid of reprisals by the religious authorities.

But before the two men could say a word about their experience on the road to Emmaus, the others—including Simon Peter—broke in with some news of their own:

"The Lord really was raised from the dead, and he has appeared to Simon."

Then, Cleopas and his friend began to relate their experience on the road to Emmaus, and told how they had recognized Jesus when he broke the bread in their presence.

A little later, during the early evening hours on that Sunday, Thomas left the group. But soon after his departure, another even more dramatic event reportedly occurred: For the first time, Jesus appeared to a significant group of his main followers—including ten apostles (minus Thomas), Cleopas, and the others who were still talking in the locked room.

"Peace be with you!" he said.

They were shocked and terrified because they thought they were seeing a ghost.

"Why are you worried?" Jesus asked.. "Why do you have doubts? Look at my hands and my feet. It's really me! Touch me and see— because a ghost doesn't have flesh and bones as you can see I do."

But because of their stunned astonishment, and a sense that what they were seeing was "too good to be true," they still couldn't quite believe.

So he offered further proof by asking them, "Do you have anything here to eat?"

Someone gave him a piece of broiled fish, and he took it and ate it in their presence.

Then, Jesus provided even *more* proof by showing them his hands again, and by revealing his wounded side. This accumulation of evidence finally convinced them that it really was their Lord—and they were overjoyed.

Again, Jesus said, "Peace be with you. Now, I'll send you on special missions, as the Father has sent me."

Then he breathed on them and, apparently in a special act of commissioning, declared: "Receive the Holy Spirit. Now, you disciples can be sure that when you are acting in the Spirit, any sins that you forgive *have already been forgiven by the Father.* And any sins that you seize or retain in the Spirit *have already been seized or retained by the Father.*"

As indicated above, Thomas—also called "Didymus," or "the Twin"—was not present during this encounter. So he was skeptical when the other disciples told him later, "We have seen the Lord!"

In fact, Thomas laid down some exceptionally strict conditions that he said had to be met before he would believe that Jesus had risen physically from the dead: "Unless I see the nail marks in his hands, and put my finger where the nails were driven, and put my hand into his side—I absolutely won't believe."

With these comments by Thomas, that first, action-packed Sunday ended—but another thirty-nine days of startling resurrection events remained.

Dealing with a Man of Doubt

Eight days later, the disciples were again sitting in their locked room—apparently still afraid of the religious authorities. But this time, Thomas was with them.

Once again, Jesus stood before them in the room and said: "Peace be with you!"

Although Jesus had already initiated a number of other face-to-face encounters with individuals or small groups, this was only his second appearance to a significantly large group of his apostles.

Jesus immediately focused on Thomas and said: "Reach your finger over here, and touch my hands. And reach your hand down here, and put it into my side. Stop doubting and believe!"

"My Lord and my God!" Thomas answered.

"Because you have seen me, you have believed?" Jesus said. "Blessed are those who do not see, yet believe."

The Scene Shifts to Galilee

Now that all of the apostles were convinced that Jesus had risen from the dead, they were ready to follow his original instructions to go to Galilee, the northern region of ancient Palestine. (Remember: Jesus had told the women at the tomb early on the morning of his Resurrection that they should tell the disciples to meet him in Galilee, where he had done much of his teaching.)

After they arrived in Galilee, which borders the Sea of Tiberias (also called the "Sea of Galilee"), Simon Peter announced to the six who where with him: "I am going fishing."

His companions included Thomas called "Didymus" ("the Twin"); Nathanael of Cana in Galilee; James the son of Zebedee; John the son of Zebedee; and two other unnamed disciples.

The others responded, "We'll come with you."

So they all set out on the water in a boat well before the sun came up—but they caught nothing.

As the sun was just breaking, they saw a figure standing on the beach, but they couldn't tell who it was.

The man called out, "Children, you don't have any fish, do you?"

"No," they answered.

Then the stranger gave them some advice: "Cast the net on the right side of the boat and you will find something."

They did as he said—and caught so many fish they weren't able to haul in the net!

Then John, son of Zebedee, who referred to himself as the "disciple Jesus loved," said to Peter: "It is the Lord!"

When Peter heard that it was the Lord, he put on his clothes—because he had stripped naked for work on the boat—and jumped into the sea and headed toward shore, which was about one hundred yards away. The other disciples followed in the boat, dragging the net full of fish.

When they reached the shore, they saw that Jesus had bread ready for them, and fish that were already cooking on a fire.

"Bring some of those fish you just caught," Jesus said.

So Simon Peter went over to the net and drew it onto the land. Even though they counted 153 fish in the net, the net was not torn.

"Come and eat some breakfast," Jesus said.

None of the disciples dared ask him, "Who are you?" because they knew he was Jesus.

Jesus proceeded to take the bread and fish and serve them—and thus began his third post-resurrection appearance to a large group of the apostles.

Peter on the Hot Seat

After they had finished their breakfast, Jesus and Simon Peter took a walk, during which Jesus asked the leader of his apostles a series of probing questions:

"Simon, son of John, are you really committed to love me more than all these other companions of yours?" Jesus asked.

"Yes, Lord," Peter replied, "you know that I love you as deeply as any friend could."

"Feed my lambs," Jesus said.

Then Jesus challenged Peter with a second question: "Simon, son of John, do you really love me with all your will?"

"Yes, Lord," Peter replied again, "you know that I love you as much as any human being could."

"Be a shepherd to my little sheep," Jesus said.

Finally Jesus posed a third question to Peter: "Simon, son of John, do you have a real personal affection for me?"

"Lord," Peter replied, "you know all things, and so you know that I have the greatest affection for you."

"Feed my little sheep," Jesus emphasized again. "And now let me speak as truthfully and as bluntly to you as I can, Peter: When you were younger, you used to bind yourself up with a belt and walk wherever you wanted. But when you grow old, you will stretch out your hands, and someone else will bind you up, and bring you where you do not wish to go."

At the time, the full import of this statement wasn't clear—though Peter and his companions were aware that Jesus was imparting to him some very painful news about the future. Later reports have confirmed that Jesus made this statement to Peter to show the kind of death he would have to suffer later for the cause of Christ.

Then Jesus capped this intense interrogation with the same command he had put to Peter at the beginning of their ministry together: "Follow me!"

At this point, Peter looked over his shoulder and saw the apostle John following them. "Lord, what about this fellow?" Peter asked.

"If I want him to remain until I come a second time to establish my kingdom, what's that to you? You just follow me!"

As a result of this statement, a rumor arose that John would not die before Jesus' Second Advent. But John, our reporter who actually heard the statement, is adamant that this wasn't the meaning. According to John, Jesus did not say that John wouldn't die—only that it was none of Peter's business if Jesus wanted John to live until his Second Coming.

A Big Gathering in Galilee

After this encounter on the seashore, Jesus met the entire group of eleven apostles on a particular mountain that he had designated in Galilee. Also, other followers of Jesus, who had gotten word about the scheduled appearance, showed up on the mountain—until more than five hundred were present.

When the eleven apostles saw him at a distance, they prostrated themselves before him and worshiped him. But some of the hundreds of observers had doubts. (Most of those who witnessed this event were still alive when reporter Paul first published his account of this event.)

Then Jesus approached and began speaking to them:

"All authority in heaven and on earth has been given to me. So go and disciple all the nations, baptizing them in the name of the Father and of the Son and of the Holy Spirit, teaching them to observe all things about which I have commanded you. And listen closely! I am with you all of the days, until the entire completion of the age."

Two Brothers

In much the same private way that he met with Peter, the risen Jesus also made a special appearance to his half brother, James. (James was Jesus' half brother because even though they had the same mother, Mary, they had different fathers—Joseph and God.)

James, along with his other brothers, was not among Jesus' followers and did not believe in him during his Galilean ministry. But James and his brothers were among the eleven apostles and Jesus' other followers who gathered together in Jerusalem just after Jesus made his last resurrection appearance.

No evidence has been uncovered indicating the place or purpose of this special resurrection appearance to James. But informed sources have suggested that there may have been at least two reasons for the meeting: first, the conversion of James so that he finally became a follower of Jesus; and second, the preparation of James for his later role as the leader of the Christian community in Jerusalem.

Back to Jerusalem

After the events in Galilee were finished, the eleven apostles and their companions traveled back to Jerusalem. There, they met again with the risen Christ. During that session, Jesus taught them more about his mission and his position as Messiah.

"These are my words, which I spoke to you while I was still with you—that all things which are written about me in the Law of Moses and the prophets and the psalms must be fulfilled," he said.

Then he opened their minds so they could understand the Scriptures.

"Thus it is written—that the Messiah should suffer and rise again from the dead on the third day," Jesus said. "Also, repentance for the forgiveness of sins must be proclaimed in the Messiah's name to all nations—beginning here in Jerusalem.

"You are witnesses of these things. Now pay attention: I am sending forth upon you the promise of my Father, which you heard about from me. For John baptized with water, but you shall be baptized in the Holy Spirit not many days from now. But you must sit here in the city until you are clothed with power from on high."

The Last Appearance—and a New Beginning

After this—on the fortieth day after his resurrection—Jesus led them all out about three-quarters of a mile in the direction of Bethany, to the Mount of Olives.

When they had all gathered together on the mount, the disciples asked him, "Lord, are you restoring the kingdom to Israel at this time?"

Jesus answered: "It is not for you to know the times or seasons that the Father has set within his own authority. But you shall receive power when the Holy Spirit has come upon you. And you shall be my witnesses, both in Jerusalem, and in all Judea and Samaria, and to the farthest parts of the earth."

Then, lifting up his hands, he blessed them. While he was in this very act of blessing them—and they were looking directly at him—he was lifted upward into a cloud, so that they could no longer see him.

While they were gazing toward heaven as he departed, two men in white garments suddenly appeared and stood beside them. "Men of Galilee," the two men said, "why are you standing here, looking toward heaven? This Jesus, who has been taken up from you into heaven, will come in the same way that you watched him go into heaven."

The group then returned from the Mount of Olives to Jerusalem with great joy. And in the days following this last appearance of Jesus— when they weren't waiting in the upper room—they were continually in the temple, praising God.

CHAPTER 6

The "What" Question—Anatomy of the Rewrite

There is a tendency among latter-day journalistic pundits to scoff at some "old-fashioned" newswriting formulas, such as the requirement that a reporter or rewrite man answer the six basic newswriting questions: "What," "Who," "When," "Where," and "How" or "Why."

Under the classic application of this formula, a breaking news story would have to answer all of the first four questions, plus at least one of the last two, in the lead (the first sentence or two). In a feature, newswriters would be cut a little more slack; but still, at least five questions, and preferably all six, would have to be answered before the concluding paragraph.

Unfortunately, a cavalier dismissal of this traditional checklist often adds up to incomplete, shoddy reporting and writing. I've noticed that in *every single newspaper* I've read in my travels to various cities in the past ten to fifteen years, some article will answer only four or fewer of these basic questions. And that includes an occasional article even in our highly touted "newspaper of record," *The New York Times*.

Usually, when a writer ignores the six-question checklist, he or she leaves out *both* of the tough final two questions: "How?" and "Why?" As a result, the reasons, purposes, or motives for the events may be omitted—and serious readers are left frustrated with a relatively shallow story.

The following chapters have been organized around the six-question framework—and this one deals with the "what?" question, or the key events that occurred during the resurrection occurrences. We'll explore *what exactly happened* by taking apart and analyzing the rewrite from the previous chapter.

An Anatomy Lesson

The finished rewrite of a news report is supposed to be smooth and readable, with as few "holes"—or unanswered questions and uncovered issues—as possible. But before the rewrite man completes the draft of a complex story, there are often many rough spots to negotiate. Myriad facts may have to be moved around, in an effort to fit them in here and there in the narrative, as one would do with a jigsaw puzzle.

To show you how the final version of the resurrection rewrite in chapter 4 came about—and how some potential conflicts in the narrative were reconciled—here is a blow-by-blow account of the sources I used and the judgment calls I had to make. The rewritten narrative from chapter 5 is reproduced here. But this time, the text is broken up into twenty-seven separate "events" to make it easier to see the "what"—or precise sequence of facts—of the story.

Also, specific source materials and other explanations are included after each event so that you can get a better picture of the underlying "anatomy" of the rewrite job. These sections include citations of specific biblical references, identification of probable eyewitnesses and other sources for the events, and explanations of the rationale for rewriting difficult passages so that they are more understandable.

Note: A number of issues are covered in later chapters—such as the identity of the characters (see the "who" chapter), and the date chosen for the events (see the "when" chapter).

The Anatomy of the Rewrite

IS THE "KING OF THE JEWS" STILL ALIVE?
A Startling Report of a Resurrection in Judea
By Matthew, Mark, Luke, John, Peter, and Paul
with William Proctor

JERUSALEM. In a truly mind-boggling turn of events, the controversial Jewish teacher and accused revolutionary, Jesus of Nazareth— who was reviled and crucified just outside the walls of Jerusalem on Friday, April 7, A.D. 30—has apparently risen from the dead and appeared to more than five hundred eyewitnesses, according to extensive interviews and research conducted by a team of six investigative reporters. The sequence of events began with a hasty burial and an alleged cover-up conspiracy involving Roman officials and local religious leaders.

A Hasty Burial

Event #1: The Burial of Jesus by Joseph of Arimathea and Nicodemus, and First Two Burial Preparations by the Women

After Jesus was crucified on that Friday, he was buried hurriedly in the late afternoon by two members of the Sanhedrin, the ruling Jewish religious council.

The men, Joseph of Arimathea and Nicodemus, had to work quickly before the arrival of the Sabbath at sundown. Under Jewish religious law, they would not have been permitted to perform burial work after that point. As a result, the preparation of the body for burial was only partially completed.

The tomb, which had never been used before and was located in a garden near the spot where the crucifixion took place, was donated by Joseph, a wealthy follower of Jesus. The other Sanhedrin member, Nicodemus, also a follower of Jesus, supplied one hundred pounds of myrrh and aloes. These spices were stuffed quickly into the shroud, which was used to wrap the dead teacher's body. Finally, the men rolled a huge circular stone in front of the entrance.

As the two men worked, Mary Magdalene and the "other" Mary—who was the mother of the apostle James the Less and his brother, Joses—showed up and took seats opposite the grave. Other women also came to the tomb at about this time.

Then, just before the Sabbath commenced at sundown, the women left to buy and prepare some, but not all, of the spices and ointments that were needed to complete the burial preparations. Finally, after the Sabbath had begun that evening, they rested in obedience to the Jewish Law.

Sources and Explanations for Event #1

The biblical sources for this event are Mark 15:42-47; Matthew 27:57–61; Luke 23:50–56; and John 19:38–42.

The purchase, preparation, and application of the spices and ointments for Jesus' burial apparently occurred in several stages: First, Nicodemus began the process with about one hundred pounds of myrrh and aloes, which were placed hurriedly on the body. Second, immediately after the burial but *before* the onset of the Sabbath, the women—who saw that more needed to be done to prepare the body—went out quickly to buy and prepare extra spices and ointments. Third, as indicated below in Event #3, Mary Magdalene, the "other" Mary, and Salome made a final purchase of spices *after* the Sabbath had ended. This additional purchase by the women may have been required because of their necessarily hurried purchases on Friday, as the Sabbath was about to begin.

None of the accounts of the condition of the empty tomb after the Resurrection—as detailed as they may be—mention any spice residue at the gravesite. The only evidence that a burial had occurred was the linen body wrappings and the napkin or head cloth. Yet the weight of spices, added to the weight of Jesus' body, would have created an unwieldy load of at least about 250 to 300 pounds. The logistics confronting any humans who tried to move such a package quietly and cleanly would have been formidable.

The Beginning of a Government Cover-up?

Event # 2: The Religious Rulers Act on Their Fears

Despite clear evidence of death and burial, Jesus' enemies, the chief priests and certain Pharisees, were still worried about him when Saturday dawned, insiders within the Sanhedrin disclosed. Even though this day was a Sabbath, when strict rules for Jews about traveling and contact with Gentiles were in force, the religious leaders arranged a meeting with Pontius Pilate, the Roman procurator of Judea.

According to these Sanhedrin sources, the religious leaders warned Pilate that when he was still alive, the "deceiver" Jesus had said, "After three days I will rise again."

"So please order his tomb to be secured against any intruders until the third day," the religious authorities urged. "Otherwise, his disciples may steal his body and tell the people that he has been raised from the dead. This last deception could be even worse than his other lies."

Pilate went along with the request, but put the burden on them to carry it out. "You have a guard," he said. "Go and make the tomb as secure as you can."

The religious leaders immediately moved to post an around-the-clock guard and put a seal on the large stone that blocked the entrance to the tomb.

Sources and Explanations for Event #2

The biblical source for this event is Matthew 27:62–66.

This meeting occurred on a Sabbath, designated here as the day after "Preparation Day," which was also the day after the Crucifixion. Although the Sabbath rules generally prohibited such encounters, the chief priests and some representatives of the Pharisees, a strict Jewish religious party, felt the situation was serious enough for them to meet with Pilate, the Roman procurator of Judea.

Spices at Sundown

Event #3: The Third Burial Preparation by the Women

Meanwhile, the executed teacher's followers were planning how to complete the burial procedures. At sundown that same Saturday, which marked the end of the Sabbath, three Jewish women, who had been long-time supporters of Jesus, bought additional spices that they planned to use to finish anointing the body. The women included:

- Mary Magdalene, who was widely reported to have been freed of seven demons by Jesus;
- Another Mary—sometimes called the "other Mary"—who was the mother of James the Less, one of Jesus' twelve top disciples, or "apostles"; and
- Salome, the wife of Zebedee and mother of two of the twelve apostles, James and John.

Sources and Explanations for Event #3

The biblical source for this event is Mark 16:1.

As indicated in the discussion under Event #1, this purchase by the women is the third step they took in preparing the body of Jesus for burial. (As it turned out, of course, the spices they purchased on Friday and again on Saturday evening were never used because by the time they finally reached the tomb, Jesus had risen.)

Event #4: Two Women View the Tomb from a Distance

Sometime just before dawn, Mary Magdalene and Mary, the mother of James the Less, walked over to take a look at the tomb. They moved rather slowly because they were carrying the spices they had bought the night before. On the way, they met Salome, who was also loaded down with spices.

But then, as dawn broke and the tomb, which was still in deep shadows, came into view, a disturbing thought struck the three women: "Who will roll the stone away from the entrance so we can prepare the body?"

At this point—according to the eyewitness testimony of all three women—an extraordinary series of events began to unfold.

Sources and Explanations for Event #4

The biblical sources are Matthew 28:1, John 20:1, and Mark 16:2–3.

The inference that the tomb was dark because it was in shadows is drawn from John 20:1. The assumption that Mary Magdalene and the "other" Mary approached together as a group of two comes from Matthew 28:1. Salome appears to have joined them at some point along the way, according to Mark 16:1–3.

An Earthquake, an Empty Tomb—and Total Terror

Event #5: The Earthquake at the Tomb

First, an earthquake struck the area, and the women were so disconcerted that they temporarily looked down and lost sight of the tomb. But when they looked up again, they saw that the very large stone had been rolled away during the earthquake.

Source for Event #5

The biblical source is Matthew 28:2.

Event #6: Mary Magdalene, One of the First Three Women to See the Open Tomb, Rushes Back to Tell the Disciples

Leaving her two companions, Mary Magdalene rushed away to tell Simon Peter and the apostle John what she perceived to be the *bad* news. Apparently thinking that the religious leaders or guards had removed the body, she was distraught when she found them.

"They have taken the Lord out of the tomb, and we don't know where they have put him!" she cried.

Then, she sought out the other apostles to tell them what she had seen.

Source and Explanations for Event #6

The biblical source is John 20:1–2.

John mentions only Mary Magdalene—a selective presentation of the facts, apparently because at this point, he wants to focus on her story and her anxieties.

Event # 7: The Guards Are Struck with Terror at the Appearance of a Single Angel, Who Converses with the Women at the Gravesite

Meanwhile, Salome and the "other" Mary, who had remained in the vicinity of the gravesite, moved closer to the tomb entrance. They soon noticed that the guards posted by the religious leaders were lying on the ground, some shaking uncontrollably, others as rigid as dead men.

As they started to enter the tomb, the women saw what had apparently triggered the guards' fright: A fearsome angelic figure in the form of a young man was sitting on the large stone at the entrance, with clothing as white as snow and an overall appearance that they could only describe as "like lightning."

Conversations with an Angel—and the First Eyewitness Resurrection Report

The angel made it clear to Salome and the "other" Mary that the earthquake had accompanied his arrival and that he was responsible for moving the stone. They were utterly amazed and astonished—and afraid as well.

But the angel took pains to calm them.

"Don't be alarmed," he said. "I know you are looking for Jesus, who was crucified. He is not here—he has risen, just as he said. Look at the place where they laid his body. Then go quickly and tell his disciples and Peter this: 'He has risen from the dead and is going ahead of you into Galilee. There you will see him, just as he told you.' Now, I have told you."

At that, Salome and the "other" Mary left the tomb, too frightened at first to tell anyone what they had seen. But soon joy overtook them, their courage returned, and they ran to tell the disciples. But their morning adventures weren't over yet.

Source and Explanations for Event #7

The biblical sources for this event are Mark 16:5–8 and Matthew 28:2–8.

The merger of the angel's words from these two sources provides a more complete picture of what he said. Also, combining the sources gives a richer sense of the evolving response of the women, from being almost as terrified as the guards, to being overjoyed and ready to share their experience with others.

Remember, the assumption of any rewrite man dealing with two competent reporters is that *both* their reports are correct, even if, at first, they seem inconsistent. The challenge is to reconcile them if they can be reconciled—and in this case, Mark and Matthew *can* be reconciled.

Event #8: Salome and the "Other" Mary Encounter the Risen Christ

According to the two women's eyewitness report, Jesus himself met them as they were en route to the disciples and said simply, "Greetings!"

They gathered about him, held on to his feet, and worshiped him. Then he reemphasized the angel's message: "Don't be afraid," he said. "Go and tell my brothers to go to Galilee. They will see me there."

Sources and Explanations for Event #8

The main biblical source is Matthew 28:9–10.

The assumption that only Salome and the "other" Mary were present at this meeting is based on the inference that Mary Magdalene had already left the other two women so that she could report to the disciples (see John 20:2).

The Cover-up Consummated

Event #9: The Guards Recover and Flee to the Religious Authorities, Who Plan a Cover-up

Sources at the Sanhedrin have disclosed that after the three women had left the tomb, the guards came to their senses and ran back to report to the chief priests all that had happened.

The chief priests and elders then devised a cover-up plan. They bribed the soldiers with a large sum of money and instructed them this way:

"You are to say, 'His disciples came during the night and stole him away while we were asleep.' If this report gets to the governor, we will satisfy him and keep you out of trouble."

The soldiers took the money and did as they were told, according to the Sanhedrin sources. It is also general public knowledge in Judea that this very story is still being widely circulated in that province of the Roman Empire.

Source for Event #9

The biblical source is Matthew 28:11–15.

Some scholars feel the soldiers were members of the Temple guard, composed mostly of Levites. Others argue they were Roman soldiers attached to the Sanhedrin. The implied threat in this passage that they might get in trouble with Pilate suggests the latter—that they were Romans.

A Second Angel

Event #10: Another Group of Women, Including Joanna, Go to the Tomb and Encounter Two Angels

As Salome and the "other" Mary proceeded on their way to the disciples—whom Mary Magdalene was already in the process of contacting—still *another* group of women arrived at the tomb with spices. These included Joanna, the wife of Herod's steward Chuza. Like the other women before them, this new group found the stone rolled away, but the stunned guards were gone by this time.

Joanna and her companions walked directly into the tomb and saw that Jesus' body was gone, according to their eyewitness report. While they were standing in the tomb wondering about this, *two* men in clothing that gleamed like lightning suddenly stood beside them.

The women were so frightened and overwhelmed that they bowed down with their faces to the ground.

But the two men said, "Why do you look for the living among the dead? He is not here. He has risen! Remember how he told you while he was still with you in Galilee: 'The Son of Man must be delivered into the hands of sinful men, be crucified and on the third day be raised again.'"

Then, the women remembered Jesus' words during his teaching ministry while he was still alive—and they rushed off to report what they had observed to the disciples.

Source for Event #10

The biblical source is Luke 24:1–8.

Skepticism and an Investigation

Event #11: The Women Tell the Disciples about the Events They Have Witnessed—but the Men Don't Believe Them

In waves, the various women—Mary Magdalene; then Salome and the "other" Mary; and finally Joanna and her group—found the eleven apostles and other disciples and told their stories. But the men didn't believe the reports because, as they said, the women's words seemed to them to be "nonsense."

Source for Event #11
The biblical source for this event is Luke 24:9–11.

Event #12: Peter and John Investigate
Peter and John, however, decided to investigate further. They both ran toward the tomb, but John says that he was faster and arrived first. He bent over, looked into the tomb, and saw linen burial wrappings—but he didn't enter.

Peter finally made it to the tomb, but he didn't linger at the entrance; he went directly inside, according to John's eyewitness report. There, he saw not only the linen wrappings that John had seen, but also a napkin or towel that had been on Jesus' head. This napkin had been rolled up and placed apart from the linen wrappings.

John says that he then followed Peter into the tomb and, like Peter, saw with his own eyes the linen wrappings as well as the separately wrapped-up head towel. As a result, unlike the other apostles and disciples, John was led to believe at least this much: that what the women had reported about the empty tomb was true.

Peter's opinions after this experience are not a matter of public record. But interviews with John have revealed that neither John nor Peter had a complete understanding of the Resurrection at this point because neither was knowledgeable about the scriptural passages supporting the idea that the Messiah must rise from the dead. These two apostles—who with James, the brother of John, were Jesus' closest companions during his preaching and teaching ministry—then returned home.

Source for Event #12
The biblical source is John 20:3–10.

Mary Magdalene's Emotional Roller Coaster

Event #13: Mary Magdalene Follows Peter and John Back to the Tomb and Encounters Two Angels

Mary Magdalene, who had followed Peter and John back to the tomb, lingered just outside the entrance after they had gone home. As she stood there, she began to cry. Still weeping, she bent over to get her first look inside the tomb—and an amazing sight awaited her.

According to her report, two angels in white were sitting on the slab where Jesus' body had been laid, one at the head and the other at the foot.

"Woman, why are you crying?" they asked her.

"They have taken my Lord away," she replied, still under the impression that Jesus' body had been stolen. "And I don't know where they have put him."

Source for Event #13

The biblical source is John 20:11–13.

Event #14: Mary Magdalene Meets Jesus—Whom She at First Mistakes for a Gardener

Before the angels could answer, Mary Magdalene turned around and saw a man, whom she thought was the gardener, standing behind her. Because her eyes were filled with tears, and also because she wasn't looking directly at him, she couldn't see him clearly.

"Woman, why are you crying?" the man said. "Who is it that you are looking for?"

"Sir, if you have carried him away, tell me where you have put him, and I will get him," Mary replied.

"Mary," the man said—and immediately Mary turned toward him and recognized him as Jesus.

"Rabboni!" she cried out in Aramaic, using a title that means "teacher."

"Do not hold on to me because I have not yet ascended to the Father," Jesus cautioned. "Instead, go to my brothers and tell them,

'I am ascending to my Father and your Father, to my God and your God.'"

Source for Event #14
The biblical source is John 20:14–17.

Event #15: Mary Magdalene Makes Her Second Report to the Disciples
So Mary Magdalene took *another* report on her experiences at the empty tomb back to the disciples. This time, however, she opened with a more upbeat message:

"I have seen the Lord!"

Then she proceeded to tell them about her encounter with the risen Jesus, including what he had said to her.

Source for Event #15
The biblical source is John 20:18.

A Secret Rendezvous

Event #16: Jesus Has a Private Meeting with Peter
Later in the day on that first Easter, Jesus made a special appearance to Peter, according to Peter himself. Because this was a highly confidential meeting, no details are available.

But knowledgeable authorities on the resurrection events have suggested that this special, private appearance may reflect a recognition of Peter's stature as leader of the twelve apostles. Also, Jesus may have felt there was a need to reaffirm Peter and make it clear that he was forgiven despite his denials at the trial of Jesus.

Finally, Peter may have needed some special instructions and encouragement because he was slated to play a decisive role in leading the early Christian community after Jesus' final departure from earth at the Ascension.

Sources and Explanations for Event #16

There are two biblical sources that refer to this meeting: Luke 24:34 and 1 Corinthians 15:5.

Details are lacking, but we can assume that Peter was ultimately the source of the account in Luke, and probably in Paul's letter to Corinth as well. The suggested purposes of the meeting are guesses based on what we know of Peter's background, his position of leadership with the apostles, and his later role in the church.

The Emmaus Road Incident

Event #17: Jesus Appears to Cleopas and One Other Disciple on the Road to Emmaus

On that same Sunday afternoon, two followers of Jesus, who were walking toward Emmaus, a village about seven miles from Jerusalem, reported another highly unusual incident.

The men—one Cleopas and an unidentified companion—were deep in conversation about the reports of an empty tomb when a stranger walking along the same road moved over and joined them. Cleopas recalled the conversation this way:

"What are you talking about on your walk?" the man asked.

"Are you the only person visiting Jerusalem who doesn't know the things that have happened around here in the last few days?" Cleopas replied.

"What things?" the stranger asked.

"Things about Jesus of Nazareth," Cleopas and his companion said, both contributing now to the conversation with the third man. "He was a prophet of God who was powerful in word and deed. Any of the people could tell you that. The chief priests and our rulers handed him over for a judgment of death, and they crucified him."

"As for us, we were hoping that Jesus was the one who would redeem Israel—even though it's now the third day since his crucifixion," they continued. "But some women from our group amazed us just a few hours ago. They came and told us they had gone to the tomb early this morning but didn't find his body. Instead, they said that they saw a vision of angels, who said he was alive.

"Then some of our men went to the tomb to check out the story. They found everything exactly as the women had said, but they did not see Jesus."

The stranger heard them out, but then responded unexpectedly with a rebuke: "How foolish you are and slow in your hearts to believe all that the prophets have spoken! Wasn't it *necessary* for the Messiah to suffer these things and then enter his glory?"

With that, the stranger proceeded to explain to them how the Scriptures, beginning with Moses and all the prophets, had actually foreshadowed Jesus as the Messiah.

As the three men approached the village of Emmaus, the stranger indicated in a polite way that he would continue on. But Cleopas and his companion insisted that he stop, saying, "Stay with us because it will be dark soon."

So the stranger joined them in the house where they were staying. As they prepared to eat, the stranger reclined at the table, took a loaf of bread, and blessed it. Then he broke it and began to hand pieces to them.

At this moment, somehow, in some inexplicable way as the loaf was being broken, their "eyes were opened up," as they put it, and they recognized that the stranger was really Jesus. Then he vanished or "became invisible"—again in some way that defied their rational explanation.

Cleopas and his friend stayed in the house for several minutes, reflecting on the incident and trying to absorb its meaning. One observation they both made: "Weren't our hearts burning within us as he spoke to us on the road and opened up the Scriptures to us?"

Realizing the potential significance of their encounter with the risen Christ, the two men decided they had to return to Jerusalem immediately to tell the other disciples. So despite the waning daylight, they headed back toward Jerusalem within the hour.

Source and Explanations for Event #17

The biblical source is Luke 24:13–33.

The two disciples' failure to recognize Jesus at first was a common phenomenon in the post-resurrection appearances (see Event #14, for example). There are a couple of possible reasons for this lack of recognition.

First, his resurrection body may have included the power to remain unrecognized at will. In this case, Jesus simply disguised himself or kept their eyes "closed" until he was ready to reveal himself.

Second, these two disciples, as well as Jesus' other followers, weren't expecting to see him again—and as every good reporter knows, expectations can play tricks on memory and perception. It may be that because Cleopas and his friend had completely failed to understand Jesus' teachings about his resurrection, they simply weren't prepared to accept the idea that a person who had been crucified and buried could still be walking around.

A Meeting with a "Ghost"

Event #18: Cleopas and His Companion Report the Emmaus Road Incident to the Eleven—and Learn about Jesus' Appearance to Peter

When Cleopas and his companion arrived in Jerusalem, they went straight to a house where the eleven apostles and some other followers of Jesus were holding a closed meeting. The doors had been locked because the disciples were afraid of reprisals by the religious authorities.

But before the two men could say a word about their experience on the road to Emmaus, the others—including Simon Peter—broke in with some news of their own:

"The Lord really was raised from the dead, and he has appeared to Simon."

Then Cleopas and his friend began to relate their experience on the road to Emmaus, and told how they had recognized Jesus when he broke the bread in their presence.

Source for Event #18

The biblical source for this event is Luke 24:33–35.

Event #19: Jesus Appears to Ten of the Apostles and Other Disciples, Including Cleopas and His Companion

A little later, during the early evening hours on that Sunday, Thomas left the group. But soon after his departure, another even more dramatic event reportedly occurred: For the first time, Jesus appeared to a significant group of his main followers—including ten apostles (minus Thomas), Cleopas, and the others who were still talking in the locked room.

"Peace be with you!" he said.

They were shocked and terrified because they thought they were seeing a ghost.

"Why are you worried?" Jesus asked. "Why do you have doubts? Look at my hands and my feet. It's really me! Touch me and see—because a ghost doesn't have flesh and bones as you can see I do."

But because of their stunned astonishment, and a sense that what they were seeing was "too good to be true," they still couldn't quite believe.

So he offered further proof by asking them, "Do you have anything here to eat?"

Someone gave him a piece of broiled fish, and he took it and ate it in their presence.

Then, Jesus provided even more proof by showing them his hands again, and by revealing his wounded side. This accumulation of evidence finally convinced them that it really was their Lord—and they were overjoyed.

Again, Jesus said, "Peace be with you. Now, I'll send you on special missions, as the Father has sent me."

Then he breathed on them and, apparently in a special act of commissioning, declared: "Receive the Holy Spirit. Now, you disciples can be sure that when you are acting in the Spirit, any sins that you forgive *have already been forgiven by the Father.* And any sins that you seize or retain in the Spirit *have already been seized or retained by the Father.*"

Sources and Explanations for Event #19

The sources for this event are Luke 24:36–43 and John 20:19–23.

Jesus' "breathing on" or "into" the disciples is reminiscent of God's "breathing into" Adam the breath of life in Genesis 2:7. In both instances, God's Spirit is activated in a special way.

My rewritten rendition of the difficult "forgiveness-of-sins" passage in John 20:23 seems to me the best way to capture the underlying assumption that only God, not men, can actually forgive or retain sins. Human beings, acting under the guidance of the Holy Spirit, are limited to *proclaiming* what God, through Christ, has already done. This position is supported by the perfect tenses ("have been forgiven" and "have been seized/retained"), which are faithful to the Greek text—and are used by the NASB translation.

Event #20: Thomas Is Skeptical

As indicated above, Thomas—also called "Didymus," or "the Twin"—was not present during this encounter. So he was skeptical when the other disciples told him later, "We have seen the Lord!"

But like his fellow apostles when Jesus had first appeared before them, Thomas was skeptical.

In fact, Thomas laid down some exceptionally strict conditions that he said had to be met before he would believe that Jesus had risen physically from the dead: "Unless I see the nail marks in his hands, and put my finger where the nails were driven, and put my hand into his side— I absolutely won't believe."

With these comments by Thomas, that first action-packed Sunday ended—but another thirty-nine days of startling resurrection events remained.

Source for Event #20

The biblical source is John 20:24–25.

Dealing With a Man of Doubt

Event #21: Jesus Appears to the Eleven Apostles, Including Thomas

Eight days later, the disciples were again sitting in their locked room—apparently still afraid of the religious authorities. But this time, Thomas was with them.

Once again, Jesus stood before them in the room and said: "Peace be with you!"

Although Jesus had already initiated a number of other face-to-face encounters with individuals or small groups, this was only his second appearance to a significantly large group of his apostles.

Jesus immediately focused on Thomas and said: "Reach your finger over here, and touch my hands. And reach your hand down here, and put it into my side. Stop doubting and believe!"

"My Lord and my God!" Thomas answered.

"Because you have seen me, you have believed?" Jesus said. "Blessed are those who do not see, yet believe."

Source for Event #21

The biblical source of this event is John 20:26–29.

The Scene Shifts to Galilee

Event #22: The Disciples Go to Galilee, Where Jesus Appears to Seven by the Sea of Tiberias

Now that all of the apostles were convinced that Jesus had risen from the dead, they were ready to follow his original instructions to go to Galilee, the northern region of ancient Palestine. (Remember, Jesus had told the women at the tomb early on the morning of his resurrection that they should tell the disciples to meet him in Galilee, where he had done much of his teaching.)

After they arrived in Galilee, which borders the Sea of Tiberias (also called the "Sea of Galilee"), Simon Peter announced to the six who where with him: "I am going fishing."

His companions included Thomas called "Didymus" ("the Twin"); Nathanael of Cana in Galilee; James the son of Zebedee; John the son of Zebedee; and two other unnamed disciples.

The others responded, "We'll come with you."

So they all set out on the water in a boat well before the sun came up—but they caught nothing.

As the sun was just breaking, they saw a figure standing on the beach, but they couldn't tell who it was.

The man called out, "Children, you don't have any fish, do you?"

"No," they answered.

Then the stranger gave them some advice: "Cast the net on the right side of the boat and you will find something."

They did as he said—and caught so many fish they weren't able to haul in the net!

Then John, son of Zebedee, who referred to himself as the "disciple Jesus loved," said to Peter: "It is the Lord!"

When Peter heard that it was the Lord, he put on his clothes—because he had stripped naked for work on the boat—and jumped into the sea and headed toward shore, which was about one hundred yards away. The other disciples followed in the boat, dragging the net full of fish.

When they reached the shore, they saw that Jesus had bread ready for them, and fish that were already cooking on a fire.

"Bring some of those fish you just caught," Jesus said.

So Simon Peter went over to the net and drew it onto the land. Even though they counted 153 fish in the net, the net was not torn.

"Come and eat some breakfast," Jesus said.

None of the disciples dared ask him, "Who are you?" because they knew he was Jesus.

Jesus proceeded to take the bread and fish and serve them—and thus began his third post-resurrection appearance to a large group of the apostles.

Source and Explanations for Event #22

The biblical source is John 21:1–14.

The failure of the disciples to recognize Jesus at first in this situation may simply have been due to their distance from the shore as well as the weak early morning light.

Peter on the Hot Seat

Event #23: Jesus Interrogates—and Restores—Peter

After they had finished their breakfast, Jesus and Simon Peter took a walk, during which Jesus asked the leader of his apostles a series of probing questions:

"Simon, son of John, are you really *committed* to love me more than all these other companions of yours?" Jesus asked.

"Yes, Lord," Peter replied, "you know that I love you as deeply as any friend could."

"Feed my lambs," Jesus said.

Then Jesus challenged Peter with a second question: "Simon, son of John, do you really love me with all your will?"

"Yes, Lord," Peter replied again, "you know that I love you as much as any human being could."

"Be a shepherd to my little sheep," Jesus said.

Finally Jesus posed a third question to Peter: "Simon, son of John, do you have a real personal affection for me?"

"Lord," Peter replied, "you know all things, and so you know that I have the greatest affection for you."

"Feed my little sheep," Jesus emphasized again. "And now let me speak as truthfully and as bluntly to you as I can, Peter: when you were younger, you used to bind yourself up with a belt and walk wherever you wanted. But when you grow old, you will stretch out your hands, and someone else will bind you up, and bring you where you do not wish to go."

At the time, the full import of this statement wasn't clear—although Peter and his companions were aware that Jesus was imparting to him some very painful news about the future. Later reports have confirmed that Jesus made this statement to Peter to show the kind of death he would have to suffer later for the cause of Christ.

Then Jesus capped this intense interrogation with the same command he had put to Peter at the beginning of their ministry together: "Follow me!"

At this point, Peter looked over his shoulder and saw the apostle John following them. "Lord, what about this fellow?" Peter asked.

"If I want him to remain until I come a second time to establish my kingdom, what's that to you? You just follow me!"

As a result of this statement, a rumor arose that John would not die before Jesus' Second Advent. But John, our reporter who actually heard the statement, is adamant that this wasn't the meaning. According to John, Jesus did not say that John wouldn't die—only that it was none of Peter's business if Jesus wanted John to live until his Second Coming.

Source and Explanations for Event #23

The biblical source is John 21:15–23.

The kind of love Jesus had in mind with the verb *love* in his first two questions was a noble, divinely inspired love (*agapao*). This kind of love typically is exercised not just through feelings, but through a moral act of the will. Then, Jesus switched to a verb suggesting a love characterized more by personal affection and friendship (*phileo*).

Was there a significance in this switch of verb forms?

The issue is complicated by the fact that Jesus and Peter were almost certainly speaking in Aramaic, the tongue of ancient Palestine, while the text we have from John is in Greek.

Still, John was there, listening to this entire interchange. So it would be logical to assume that in writing, he would have chosen Greek words that reflected as precisely as possible the sense in Aramaic of Jesus' questions and Peter's answers.

As a professional interviewer myself, I feel certain that there was good reason for John to use different Greek words for "love" and to report slightly varied forms of Jesus' three questions.

As a number of scholars have suggested, Jesus was using this occasion to "restore" Peter. Most likely, then, the choice of three questions wasn't accidental, since they mirrored Peter's three denials—and in effect gave him a second chance to show his loyalty.

But at the same time, Jesus appears to be using this encounter to probe the depths of Peter's commitment to him and to the fledgling church. He must have wanted to know if Peter was totally "sold out" to him, and if he loved him in every respect. Such an unswerving faith was essential for a man who was expected to assume the leadership of the

Christian community immediately after Jesus' last resurrection appearance and his Ascension.

Among other things, Jesus had to know if Peter loved him more than "these"—probably meaning his close friends who were present. Jesus knew that Peter was excessively "other-directed," or peer-oriented. He wanted desperately to be accepted and liked by others. Yet this gregarious tendency could conflict with the need for a supreme commitment to principle and to Christ himself.

Peter's three denials of Christ, for example, probably arose not just from fear or a failure of courage, but also from an unwillingness to be rejected by others as an outsider. A similar character weakness appears in Paul's criticism of Peter (Cephas) in Galatians 2:11ff.: There, Paul takes Peter to task for being hypocritical in trying to identify with both the circumcision party and with Paul's anticircumcision position.

Yet the kind of leadership that Jesus expected Peter to exercise—especially in the very first months of the church in Jerusalem—would require him at times to stand alone and become the primary target for persecution and attack.

As if to punctuate this point—and to alert Peter to the need to guard against his weakness—Jesus mildly rebuked him at the end of their conversation in John 21:21ff., as he caught the apostle in the act of comparing himself too much with John.

A Big Gathering in Galilee

Event #24: The Appearance on the Mountain to More Than Five Hundred Disciples, Including the Eleven, and the Proclamation of the Great Commission

After this encounter on the seashore, Jesus met the entire group of eleven apostles on a particular mountain that he had designated in Galilee. Also, other followers of Jesus, who had gotten word about the scheduled appearance, showed up on the mountain—until more than five hundred were present.

When the eleven disciples saw him at a distance, they prostrated themselves before him and worshiped him. But some of the hundreds of observers had doubts. (Most of those who witnessed this event were still alive when reporter Paul first published his account of this event.)

Then Jesus approached and began speaking to them:

"All authority in heaven and on earth has been given to me. So go and disciple all the nations, baptizing them in the name of the Father and of the Son and of the Holy Spirit, teaching them to observe all things about which I have commanded you. And listen closely! I am with you all of the days, until the entire completion of the age."

Sources and Explanations for Event #24

The biblical sources are 1 Corinthians 15:6 and Matthew 28:16–20.

There is some disagreement about whether the appearance to the five hundred, as reported by Paul, coincided with the Great Commission, as recorded by Matthew. I tend to side with those who advocate combining the accounts—but the accounts of Matthew and Paul can still be reconciled if they are treated as separate events.

A common argument for merging the two events is that the "eleven" in Matthew's narrative should be distinguished from the "some" who doubted. In other words, the eleven apostles were on the mountain *in addition to* an undetermined number of other disciples (more than five hundred, according to Paul).

If we assume that only the apostles were present at the Great Commission, the most logical reading of Matthew would suggest that some of the eleven were still doubting him at this point. That seems unlikely since the eleven had all been exposed to convincing appearances by Christ, and in light of the clear implication in John 20:19–29 that all the eleven apostles did believe.

In the Great Commission, I have used the verb *disciple* rather than the traditional "make disciples of." This seems the best rendition of the Greek *matheteuo*—even though in English, the verb *to disciple* is considered archaic by modern dictionaries. (But there is evidence that "to disciple" is in the process of being revived: Many contemporary evangelical Christians use the word as a verb in precisely this way—to emphasize the training and mentoring of new believers.)

Two Brothers

Event #25: Jesus Appears to James, His Half Brother

In much the same private way that he met with Peter, the risen Jesus also made a special appearance to his half brother, James. (James was Jesus' half brother because even though they had the same mother, Mary, they had different fathers—Joseph and God.)

James, along with his other brothers, was not among Jesus' followers and did not believe in him during his Galilean ministry. But James and his brothers were among the eleven apostles and Jesus' other followers who gathered in Jerusalem just after Jesus made his last resurrection appearance.

No evidence has been uncovered indicating the place or purpose of this special resurrection appearance to James. But informed sources have suggested that there may have been at least two reasons for the meeting: first, the conversion of James so that he finally became a follower of Jesus; and second, the preparation of James for his later role as the leader of the Christian community in Jerusalem.

Sources and Explanations for Event #25

These are the biblical sources for this event, in chronological order: John 7:5; 1 Corinthians 15:7; Acts 1:14; and Acts 15:1ff.

The sequence of James's spiritual progress from unbeliever, to believer, to leader of the Jerusalem church is evident in the above verses. The possible reasons given in the rewrite for the special resurrection appearance to James are based on inferences from those verses.

Again, if the "rewrite man" could have questioned Luke, John, Paul—and even James—in more depth, he might have come up with more details about James's meeting with his risen brother. On the other hand, the details may have been omitted because this meeting was intended to be completely private.

Back to Jerusalem

Event #26: Jesus Appears to the Eleven in Jerusalem—and Tells Them to Wait There for the Holy Spirit

After the events in Galilee were finished, the eleven apostles and their companions traveled back to Jerusalem. There, they met again with the risen Christ. During that session, Jesus taught them more about his mission and his position as Messiah.

"These are my words, which I spoke to you while I was still with you—that all things which are written about me in the Law of Moses and the prophets and the psalms must be fulfilled," he said.

Then he opened their minds so they could understand the Scriptures.

"Thus it is written—that the Messiah should suffer and rise again from the dead on the third day," Jesus said. "Also, repentance for the forgiveness of sins must be proclaimed in the Messiah's name to all nations—beginning here in Jerusalem.

"You are witnesses of these things. Now pay attention: I am sending forth upon you the promise of my Father, which you heard about from me. For John baptized with water, but you shall be baptized in the Holy Spirit not many days from now. But you must sit here in the city until you are clothed with power from on high."

Sources and Explanations for Event #26

The biblical sources are Luke 24:44–49 and Acts 1:3–5.

There is some disagreement about whether these two passages refer to the same event, and also about the point at which this meeting ends and the next (Event #27) begins. In any event, the rewrite is consistent with the various texts.

The Last Appearance—and a New Beginning

Event #27: Jesus Appears to the Eleven and Other Followers for the Last Time—and the Resurrection Appearances Culminate in the Ascension

After this—on the fortieth day after his resurrection—Jesus led his apostles and a number of other followers to a place on the Mount of Olives, about three-quarters of a mile in the direction of Bethany.

When they had all gathered together on the mount, the disciples asked him, "Lord, are you restoring the kingdom to Israel at this time?"

Jesus answered: "It is not for you to know the times or the seasons that the Father has set within his own authority. But you shall receive power when the Holy Spirit has come upon you. And you shall be my witnesses, both in Jerusalem, and in all Judea and Samaria, and to the farthest parts of the earth."

Then, lifting up his hands, he blessed them. While he was in this very act of blessing them—and they were looking directly at him—he was lifted upward into a cloud, so that they could no longer see him.

While they were gazing toward heaven as he departed, two men in white garments suddenly appeared and stood beside them. "Men of Galilee," the two men said, "why are you standing here, looking toward heaven? This Jesus, who has been taken up from you into heaven, will come in the same way that you watched him go into heaven."

The group then returned from the Mount of Olives to Jerusalem with great joy. And in the days following this last appearance of Jesus—when they weren't waiting in the upper room—they were continually in the temple, praising God.

Sources and Explanations for Event #27

The biblical sources for this event are Luke 24:50–53 and Acts 1:6–14.

The Mount of Olives lay on the same slope as Bethany, though Bethany itself was about one and one-half miles east of Jerusalem. Most likely, the group at the Ascension included the eleven apostles; the women who had been following Jesus and who had witnessed his resurrection appearances; Jesus' four half brothers (James, Joseph, Simon, and Judas); Jesus' mother, Mary; Joseph Barsabbas; Mathias, who was chosen later to replace Judas Iscariot; and perhaps some additional followers (see Acts 1:13–14, 21–23; Matthew 13:55–56).

* * * *

This "anatomy" should provide you with a better idea of the "what" of the rewrite—including the sources and sequence of the facts in the merged narrative. Next, we move on to the "who" of the story, or a more detailed description of the different characters who appear in the resurrection events.

CHAPTER 7

The "Who" Question—Personality Profiles of the Major Newsmakers

When a reporter is writing an events-oriented story like the Resurrection Report, there is often a tendency to focus on the action and forget about the personalities. But that's a big mistake.

The more a reader knows about the conflicts, struggles, and suffering of the people in the story, the more he or she will be able to understand the events and get involved in the drama. Personalities who are portrayed sympathetically are personalities who come across as *real*, and action that involves a strong element of human interest is action that truly comes alive.

So good journalistic action narratives, like good novels, should *always* clearly identify the people in the story. Whenever possible, they should go even further—and present the reader with fleshed-out, three-dimensional personalities.

Typically, a newspaper reporter who is dealing with the "who" of his story must at least provide full names, titles, ages, and a few other identifying characteristics, such as relevant background information. If the journalist comes up short on his identifications, he is likely to have his copy thrown back by the editor for further work.

A feature writer or journalistic book writer should go even further in describing key personalities. For example, he might mention something about the newsmaker's personal history and any distinctive personality traits. Also, in either a news story or a feature, one or more of the main newsmakers may be so important that they rate a "sidebar" or personality profile, a separate article that focuses primarily on their backgrounds and traits.

Information about the names and many other identifying features of the main characters are available in the New Testament records—though it sometimes requires digging to uncover them. In addition, church history and tradition have preserved some possible background information about a few of the personalities.

So who *are* these "newsmakers" that we have been referring to in the Resurrection Report?

There are at least twenty-six named or clearly identified individuals who were involved in the resurrection events, and hundreds of anonymous eyewitnesses and other participants. The next section focuses on short profiles of the twenty-six identifiable or "named" newsmakers, while the final section provides some background on the many "unnamed" newsmakers.

The Named Newsmakers

Newsmaker #1: Jesus of Nazareth

Jesus, the risen Christ, is obviously the main character in the resurrection events. Without him, there wouldn't be any news! For more on his preexistence, birth, life, teachings, and death, see the expanded reports by Matthew, Mark, Luke, and John in their Gospels.

Newsmaker #2: Mary Magdalene

Mary Magdalene, who was probably from the town of Magdala on the western coast of the Sea of Galilee, between Tiberias and Capernaum, had been healed by Jesus through the casting out of seven demons. She was also one of the women who contributed out of her private means to the support of Jesus and his disciples (Luke 8:1–3). There is *no* biblical evidence, by the way, to suggest that she was a "loose woman," or to link her to the woman caught in adultery.

As one of the first to see the open tomb and the first to report to the disciples on Easter morning, Mary Magdalene was one of the primary participants in the unfolding resurrection drama.

Newsmaker #3: Peter (also known as "Cephas," "Simon," and "Simon, son of John")

For Peter's background and bio, see the description in chapter 3 on the resurrection reporters.

Newsmaker #4: John, Son of Zebedee

For the background on John, the son of Zebedee and brother of James, see the description in chapter 3 on the resurrection reporters.

Newsmaker #5: The "Other" Mary

The mother of James the Less (one of the original twelve disciples) and of Joseph is also often referred to as the "other" Mary (see Mark 15:40 and Matt. 27:56).

In addition, she seems also to have been the "Mary, [wife] of Clopas," mentioned in John 19:25. Early church historians further identify this Clopas as the brother of the Joseph who was the husband of Mary, the mother of Jesus. If this is true, the "other" Mary would have been the sister-in-law of Jesus' mother.

As an observer at the Crucifixion, the burial of Christ, and his Resurrection, the "other" Mary played a big role in Christ's passion and the resurrection events.

Newsmaker #6: Salome

Salome was the wife of Zebedee and the mother of the "Boanerges" ("Sons of Thunder"), James and John (to see this connection, compare Mark 15:40 and Matt. 27:56).

Salome may also have been the sister of Mary, the mother of Jesus (see the reference to "His mother's sister" in John 19:25). If this is true, James and John would not only have been two of Jesus' three closest followers (Peter was the third), but also his first cousins.

Newsmaker #7: Joanna

Joanna, who was one of the women who reported the empty tomb to the apostles, contributed personally to the support of Jesus and his disciples (Luke 8:1–3). She also was the wife of Chuza, Herod's steward. As the manager of the political ruler's holdings, the steward would probably have been quite wealthy. Some have also identified Chuza with the royal official whose son was healed by Jesus in John 4:46ff.

Newsmaker #8: First Angel

One angel, or "young man," is mentioned in the appearance described in Mark 16:2–8 and Matthew 28:5–6. (But see below, under "Newsmaker #9: Second Angel.")

Newsmaker #9: Second Angel

Two angels (or two men in "dazzling apparel") made the news in three of the resurrection events: (1) the early appearance to the women in Luke 24:1–8; (2) the appearance to Mary Magdalene in John 20:11–18; and (3) the appearance to the apostles and their companions just after the Ascension in Acts 1:9–12.

Although each of these angels may have been a different individual, similar accounts elsewhere in Scripture seem to suggest an "economy of supernatural force," with a particular angel performing a series of similar tasks (for example, see Gabriel's role with Zacharias and Mary in Luke 1). So it's possible that the two here would have been assigned the specific task of overseeing all the resurrection events—almost as Jesus' "honor guard."

Newsmaker #10: Thomas

Thomas, also called "Didymus" ("Twin"), showed considerable courage and initiative when he told Jesus he was ready to go to the tomb of Lazarus and, if need be, die there with his master (John 11:1ff.). Also, he was quick to raise questions when he didn't understand a theological point (see the interchange in John 14:5).

Although we remember him as "doubting Thomas" because of his deep skepticism about the Resurrection, his doubts seem no more reprehensible than those of some of the other apostles who couldn't quite believe the first time they actually saw the risen Christ (see Luke 24:41).

Later church tradition says that Thomas went on missionary travels to Persia (Iran), Parthia, and India. In fact, a Christian community on the west coast of India still claims Thomas as its founder.

Newsmaker #11: Cleopas

Cleopas, one of the two men who encountered the risen Christ on the road to Emmaus (Luke 24:13–32), seems to have maintained close contacts with the apostles (see Luke 24:33–35). But nothing more is known about him.

Newsmaker #12: James, the Half Brother of Jesus

See Matthew 13:55 for the list of Jesus' four half brothers. For more on this James, see the discussion in chapter 6 under the subsection, "Two Brothers" (Event #25).

Note: The assumption in our rewrite is that James, Joseph, Simon, and Judas (see the following three "newsmakers") were the sons of Joseph and Mary (Jesus' mother), and that they were born *after* Jesus.

Two other theories have also been proposed. The first says that the brothers listed in Matthew 13:55 were born to Joseph in an earlier marriage. The problem is that there is no evidence to support this position in Scripture. Also, this view could create problems for Jesus' messianic position as eldest who would have been heir to the throne of David on Joseph's side of the family.

A second theory is that the "brothers" in this passage were actually Jesus' cousins. It is true that the Greek word *adelphos* can mean not only a brother, but also a close kinsman or relative. The argument here is that these four were actually sons of Clopas or Alphaeus, who by some traditions was the husband of a sister of Mary, Jesus' mother.

Both of these second two theories seem to strain the clear import of the Gospel record. As you will recall from chapters 1 and 2, we are assuming that the Gospel accounts should be read at face value, as pieces of first-century newswriting. The plain words of Matthew 13:53–56 (as well as Matt. 12:46–50 and other passages) establish an explicit link between Jesus' mother, Mary, and people identified as his "brothers" and "sisters." There is no mention of other ties of kinship.

Newsmaker #13: Joseph, the Half Brother of Jesus

See Matthew 13:55 and Acts 1:14 for this Joseph's shift from nonbeliever to follower of Christ. Also, see the discussion under Newsmaker #12 above.

Newsmaker #14: Simon, the Half Brother of Jesus

See the discussion under Newsmaker #12 above.

Newsmaker #15: Judas, the Half Brother of Jesus

See the discussion under Newsmaker #12 above.

By some traditions, this Judas wrote the New Testament book of Jude, probably in the second half of the first century, after the fall of Jerusalem to the Roman troops. In the first verse of the epistle, the author introduces himself as "Judas" (or "Jude"), a bond servant of Jesus Christ and the brother of James.

Newsmaker #16: Joseph Barsabbas

Joseph, called Barsabbas, was one of the two "finalists" to fill the position that was left vacant by the death of Judas Iscariot as one of the twelve apostles. A requirement for this role was that he had to have been with Christ from the beginning of his ministry through his Ascension (see Acts 1:21–23).

Newsmaker #17: Matthias

Matthias was the other finalist for the apostolic position left vacant by Judas Iscariot—and he was the one finally selected by lot (see Acts 1:21–26).

The third- and fourth-century church historian, Eusebius of Caesarea said that Matthias was also one of the large group of believers, about seventy in number, whom Jesus sent out to heal the sick and declare the coming of the kingdom of God (see Luke 10:1).

Newsmaker #18: James, Son of Zebedee

This apostle was the brother of the apostle John, one of the resurrection reporters. James, John, and Peter had the closest personal relationship to Jesus, and were the only ones present with him at such major events as the Transfiguration and Christ's special prayer time at the Garden of Gethsemane. (Also, remember the possible blood tie that may have linked Jesus, James and John. See the discussion under "Newsmaker #6.")

Jesus gave James and his brother the nickname "Boanerges" ("Sons of Thunder"), probably because of their fiery dispositions. They once recommended to Jesus that he destroy a village that had rejected the gospel (Luke 9:54).

James and John both wanted to be the greatest apostles and sit at Jesus' left and right hands in his kingdom—but Jesus said no (see Mark 10:35–41). In fact, he told them that they would drink the "cup" he had to drink—a reference to Jesus' crucifixion and James's execution.

James was put to death by Herod Agrippa I in Jerusalem in about A.D. 44 (see Acts 12:1ff.).

Newsmaker #19: Andrew

Andrew, one of the twelve apostles and the brother of Peter, was a disciple of John the Baptist before he began to follow Jesus. Originally from Bethsaida in Galilee, he later lived and worked as a fisherman with Peter in Capernaum, which lay on the northern coast of the Sea of Galilee.

Andrew is the one who initially introduced Peter to Christ (John 1:42). Later, the two of them were called by Jesus to join him in his ministry, and they immediately left their nets and followed him (Mark 1:16–18).

Also, with the apostle Philip, Andrew brought a group of Greeks to Jesus (John 12:20–22). It has been said that Andrew's actions with both Peter and the Greeks demonstrate that he was the first home missionary *and* the first foreign missionary.

Andrew also had a strong interest in eschatology, or the theology of the last days and eventual return of Christ, and he questioned Jesus about such issues in Mark 13:3–4. He was present at several of Jesus' resurrection appearances, as well as the Ascension.

According to tradition, Andrew was crucified in Achaia in Greece.

Newsmaker #20: Philip

The apostle Philip, who, like Peter and Andrew, was originally from Bethsaida, brought Nathanael (Bartholomew) to Jesus (John 1:44). Also, he made the first contact with the Greeks in John 12:21 and teamed with Andrew to bring them to Jesus.

A practical, down-to-earth man, Philip was puzzled about how to supply food for five thousand people, until Jesus showed him the miraculous solution (John 6:5). Although he obviously lacked understanding,

Philip did display a desire to deepen his spiritual experience when he asked Jesus to see the Father (John 14:8).

Caution: Philip the apostle was *not* the same person as Philip the evangelist—one of the seven believers chosen to help the twelve apostles, who were overwhelmed with work in the early church (Acts 6:5). This other Philip (the evangelist) is the man who witnessed to the Ethiopian eunuch (Acts 8:26–40), and who lived with his four prophetess-daughters in Caesarea (see Acts 21:8 for a further reference).

According to later church tradition, Philip the apostle carried his ministry to Galatia in Turkey, and he may even have traveled to the land of the Gauls in France. He was said to have been buried in Hieropolis in Galatia.

Newsmaker #21: Nathanael (Bartholomew)

Nathanael, who was from Cana in Galilee, was one of the seven disciples who met the risen Christ on the shores of the Sea of Galilee (John 21:1ff.). He was originally brought by the apostle Philip to Christ (John 1:45–46). At this first meeting with Jesus, Nathanael showed some skepticism, but Jesus quickly convinced him by demonstrating supernatural insight into Nathanael's identity.

His other name, "Bartholomew," means "son of Ptolemy."

Church tradition says that Nathanael, like Thomas, took the gospel to India.

Newsmaker #22: Matthew (Levi)

For a detailed personality profile of Matthew, who is one of the resurrection reporters, see his biographical sketch in chapter 3.

Newsmaker #23: James "the Less," Son of Alphaeus

Little is known about this apostle. His importance for the Resurrection relates to the fact that he was present for several of Jesus' major appearances. Also, he is the son of the "other" Mary, who played such a large role in the resurrection events.

Since both James the Less and Matthew were "sons of Alphaeus" (Mark 2:14), the two men may have been brothers—if the reference is to the same Alphaeus.

Newsmaker #24: Simon the Zealot (Simon the Cananean)

Simon the Zealot, also known as Simon the Cananean, has been linked to the revolutionary political movement of the Zealots. The original leader, Judas the Galilean, led a revolt against Rome in A.D. 6 to oppose giving tribute to Caesar. Even though the Romans quashed Judas' uprising, his spiritual heirs continued their armed opposition right up to their final defeat at Masada in A.D. 73.

If Simon did indeed begin as a political revolutionary, his transition to *spiritual* revolutionary obviously must have required some adjustments. But apparently, since he was present at all the resurrection appearances with the other apostles—and continued waiting with them for the Holy Spirit after the Ascension—his transformation must have been complete.

Some traditions hold that this Simon went to Spain and perhaps even to England. The second-century church historian Hegesippus, quoted in part by the later historian Eusebius of Caesarea, reported that Simon the Zealot was the same man as Simeon—who was the son of Clopas and the successor to James as the head of the church in Jerusalem.

Newsmaker #25: Judas, Son of James (Also Known as Thaddaeus or Lebbaeus)

The apostle Judas, son of James, was also known as "Thaddaeus" (Mark 3:18) and perhaps "Lebbaeus" (Matt. 10:3), both names probably being affectionate nicknames. The fourth- and fifth-century Christian translator Jerome believed that Thaddaeus, Lebbaeus, and Judas, son of James, were the same man.

"Thaddaeus" may be linked to the Aramaic word for "breast," a connection that suggests warm, affectionate friendship. "Lebbaeus," which has been eliminated from most contemporary translations because of questions about the text, is related to the Hebrew word for "heart." (Matt. 10:3 in the classic King James Version reads in part: "And Lebbaeus, whose surname was Thaddeus.")

This Judas, son of James, asked the last recorded *direct* question to Jesus in the upper room before the disciples went with Christ to the Garden of

Gethsemane: "Lord, what then has happened that You are going to disclose Yourself to us, and not to the world?" (John 14:22, NASB).

Some believe that this Judas was the son of James (Zebedee) the apostle—a relationship that would also make Judas the nephew of the resurrection reporter John. He has been linked by tradition to missionary work with King Abgar of Edessa. Also, the early Christian historian, Eusebius of Caesarea, identified Judas as one of the seventy believers who were sent out by Jesus to proclaim the gospel and minister to the sick (Luke 10:1ff.).

Newsmaker #26: Mary, Mother of Jesus

It's unclear which of the resurrection appearances Mary witnessed—or for that matter, if she witnessed any at all. But she is mentioned as being at the foot of the cross with John (John 19:25–27), and also with the apostles just after the Ascension (Acts 1:14). It seems likely she would have been present for at least one of Jesus' post-resurrection appearances—with the Ascension being the strongest candidate.

The Unnamed Newsmakers

In addition to these resurrection newsmakers who can be identified, there are also a number who are harder to pin down.

For example, there are the "chief priests," "Pharisees," "elders," and "guard" who were involved in trying to secure the tomb and body of Jesus from the feared theft by the disciples, and then in the cover-up conspiracy after Jesus' body had disappeared. Most likely, Nicodemus and Joseph of Arimathea, the members of the Sanhedrin who buried Jesus, were privy in some way—either personally or through informants—to the discussions of this group.

The "chief priests" may have included Caiaphas, the high priest at the time of the Resurrection. (His tenure in office was from 18 to 36 A.D.). Also, Annas, Caiaphas's father-in-law, had been deposed as high priest in A.D. 15, but he apparently continued to exercise some power (see Luke 3:2 and Acts 4:6).

The office of "high" or "chief" priest seems to have been something of a revolving door in those days, with many people associated with the office at one time or another. Luke says in Acts 4:6, for instance, that a "John" and an "Alexander," who were of high priestly "descent," were among those who heard the case in the Sanhedrin against Peter and John.

Another anonymous character is that second disciple who accompanied Cleopas on the road to Emmaus. And then there are the unnamed "women" who observed some of the early resurrection events, and the "disciples" other than the eleven apostles who often seemed to be in the company of more prominent followers of Jesus.

Finally, perhaps the most important unnamed group of newsmakers include the more than five hundred eyewitnesses at one resurrection appearance, which Paul mentions in 1 Corinthians 15. As we have seen, this group may have been present at the proclamation of the Great Commission in Matthew 28:19–20, or they may have been at another rally which is not recorded elsewhere in the New Testament.

In any case, their experience was extremely important in Paul's eyes because many of these people who had seen the risen Christ were alive as he wrote. Paul's assumption seems to be that if there had been any doubt about the validity of the Resurrection, they would have spoken up. In Paul's mind, they were solid proof of the central event of the faith.

So now, we have a better idea of the "who" and the "what" of the Resurrection. The next main question a good reporter would ask and investigate relates to the timing of the events—or the "when" question.

CHAPTER 8

The "When" Question—
The Timing of
the Resurrection

The "when" question that confronts a journalist evaluating the Resurrection is fairly straightforward: On what date did the resurrection of Christ occur?

A secondary "when" question depends directly on the first: When did the resurrection appearances end and the Ascension of Christ occur?

As you can see from the first paragraph of the resurrection rewrite in chapter 5, the date I have chosen for the Crucifixion is Friday, April 7, A.D. 30. This means that the Resurrection took place two days later, on Sunday, April 9 (Easter). By this chronology, the resurrection appearances would have ended forty days from Easter, with the Ascension, on May 19 of that year.

But how do we arrive at these dates?

The Debates over the Dates

Debates about the dates of the Crucifixion and Resurrection have popped up because of some uncertainties about how specific dates were calculated in first-century Judea.

Also, scholars have questioned how John's Gospel report on the timing of the passion relates to those of Matthew, Mark, and Luke—and whether the accounts can be reconciled.

It's helpful to deal with the dating of the Resurrection in terms of three issues:

- The time Jesus and his disciples ate the Last Supper—and whether this was really a Passover meal.
- The day and year of the Resurrection.
- The length of Christ's stay in the tomb.

In more detail, here some thoughts on each of these three issues.

Issue # 1: The Timing of the Last Supper

The Synoptic Gospels—Matthew, Mark, and Luke—are clear that Jesus ate the regular, traditional Passover meal.

This meal was always prepared and served at twilight (see Exod. 12:6), on the fourteenth day of Nisan, the first month of the Jewish calendar (see Exod. 12:3–6, 18; Luke 22:15).

Because each new day began for the Jews at sundown, the Passover meal would actually be finished later that night, on Nisan 15, which was the first day of the Feast of Unleavened Bread (see Matt. 26:17, 20; Mark 14:12, 17; and Luke 22:7, 14). Then, the Feast of Unleavened Bread would continue for seven days. Many times in the Scripture, the two festivals are presented as one eight-day festival.

If Jesus did indeed eat the Passover, then he was *also crucified* on Nisan 15—or the morning following the Passover meal, after the sun had come up. (Again, remember that for the Jews, each new day began at sundown. So Jesus and the disciples ate the Passover and he was crucified on the same day, according to the Jewish calendar.)

The accounts in John's Gospel have caused some controversy among scholars, some of whom feel that John says that Jesus and the disciples did *not* eat the regular Passover meal at the Last Supper. Instead, the argument goes, they were having a preliminary meal, one day before the regular Passover feast.

But an uncomplicated, literal-minded reporter has fewer difficulties with John's report. Here are some of the supposed problems, with suggested "journalistic" solutions:

- John starts off John 13:1 with the phrase "before the Passover Feast" (John 13:1) and then, briefly refers to Jesus' thoughts about his departure from the world and his love for his disciples. After that, John embarks on his description of the Last Supper.

Some have argued that the use of the word "before" should indicate that this *entire meal* (the Last Supper) was served and eaten before the regular Passover meal, which would have been scheduled for the following day.

But this interpretation doesn't make sense from John's clear, unequivocal language. Most newspaper readers would assume that John is using the word *before* to introduce the short section indicating Jesus' thoughts prior to the Passover meal. Then, John moves directly into the Passover meal itself.

- In describing Jesus' words to Judas at the supper, John first quotes Jesus as saying, "What you are about to do, do quickly" (John 13:27–29). Then, the disciples speculate that Jesus was telling Judas to buy the food that was needed for the "feast."

The argument that some scholars make is that the disciples must have thought Judas was going out to shop for the Passover meal. In this case, the argument goes, the supper they were eating could not have been the Passover.

But again, an astute newspaper reader might ask, "Why was Jesus hurrying Judas if the Passover meal was scheduled for the next day? Why couldn't Judas have gone shopping after a leisurely Last Supper and a good night's sleep?"

The probable answer: The reason the disciples thought Judas might be shopping—and had to do it quickly—was that they were already in the middle of the Passover meal. If he didn't put a move on, they would be finished before he returned!

- Another objection raised to the traditional belief that the Last Supper was the Passover meal is that John said that the hearing held by Pilate took place on "the day of Preparation of Passover Week" (John 19:14).

The argument is that the "Preparation Day" here must refer to the day before the beginning of the Passover feast. If this interpretation is accepted, the Passover meal could not have been the same as the meal eaten as the Last Supper.

The problem with this argument is that the Friday before *every* Sabbath was called the "Preparation Day." So why not just use the term Preparation Day for Friday in this case?

In short, there seems no point in choosing an interpretation of John that must conflict with the other Gospel reporters—when we have available a perfectly good interpretation that is *not* in conflict.

Again, the uncomplicated mind of the ordinary newspaper reader or reporter might think like this:

"Why assume that a report in *The New York Times* is likely to conflict with one in the *Daily News* or *The Washington Post*? Why not just assume a consistent or noncontradictory reading—unless you have solid evidence to the contrary?"

Certainly, as we have already seen, a rewrite man dealing with several competent reporters would assume that they were feeding him accurate information unless there was good cause to believe otherwise.

- Finally, John writes that the Jews did not enter Pilate's palace for Jesus' judicial proceedings because they wanted "to avoid ceremonial uncleanness" in order "to be able to eat the Passover" (John 18:28).

Some concerned scholars say that this passage must mean that the Passover feast came *after* the Last Supper of Jesus and the disciples. After all, the Last Supper had already been eaten when the Jews expressed their concern about defilement (see John 13:2).

But again, an alert reader or rewrite man might first ask a couple of pointed questions: "Did these Jewish leaders eat other meals during the Passover festival?" Also, "What exactly does it mean to 'eat the Passover'?"

The answers:

First, of course they ate other meals! The Feast of Unleavened Bread, which was directly linked to Passover, went on for an entire week and involved many meals.

Second, the phrase "eat the Passover" or "eat the festival" is used in other contexts to refer to *all* the meals of the festival period (see 2 Chron. 30:22). Also, when John uses the term *Passover,* he typically refers to the entire Passover festival (see, for example, John 2:13, 2:23, 6:4, 11:55, and 12:1). In other words, when you let the biblical text give you its own definitions and usages, the answer to a seemingly tough passage can't be too far behind.

What can we conclude from this little exercise?

Just that it is often best to read the Bible as you would your daily newspaper. Take the words at face value. Don't assume the need to find hidden meanings or come up with arcane interpretations. Let the text speak for itself and provide its own definitions. And if there is a reasonable way to reconcile accounts, choose consistency, not inconsistency.

The Bible in general—and the passion and resurrection accounts in particular—were written primarily for the average man or woman. They were *not* drafted as an intellectual exercise or game board for scholars. When we get away from straightforward reading and interpretation, we are almost certain to get into big trouble.

As for the "Passover Problem," my conclusion as a simple-minded reporter and rewrite man is, quite predictably, rather simple: It's *obvious* that Jesus ate the Passover, and equally obvious that there is no contradiction between John and the other Gospel writers.

Now, let's move on to the second major "when" issue—the day and year of the Resurrection.

Issue #2: The Day and Year of the Resurrection

Finding the day and year of the Resurrection depends directly on our conclusion about Issue #1—that Jesus and his disciples did indeed eat the Passover meal.

Here is the reasoning: Since the Last Supper was a Passover meal, the meal must have been prepared beginning on Nisan 14. Jesus and the apostles would have eaten that evening, which after sundown turned into Nisan 15. Also, the arrest and trials of Jesus would have taken place during the night of Nisan 15, and his crucifixion would have started after daybreak, still on Nisan 15.

But in terms of our calendar, on what day and year would all this have taken place?

Almost all scholars agree—and the Gospels are quite clear—that the Crucifixion took place on a Friday; Jesus lay in the tomb on Saturday (the Sabbath); and he rose from the dead on the third day, Sunday.

The challenge, then, is first to find a reasonable range of years during which the Resurrection might have occurred. Then, we must pick a a particular year within that range when Nisan 15 fell on a Friday.

First, to find a range of years that could provide us with some candidates to date the Resurrection, we have to begin with Christ's birth. We know from the accounts in Matthew 2 that Herod the Great was alive when Jesus was born. We also know from outside historical sources, including the Jewish-Roman historian Josephus, that Herod died in April of 4 B.C. So Jesus must have been born at some point earlier than that (but probably not before about 6–7 B.C., according to most scholars).

Next, we know that Jesus was about thirty years old when he began his ministry (Luke 3:23). So adding about thirty years from the approximate time of his birth, say 5 B.C., we end up with about A.D. 26–27 as the time for the beginning of Christ's ministry. Of course, the beginning point could have been a couple of years later since the Bible says he was "about" thirty when he started his ministry.

The exact length of Jesus' ministry is uncertain. But the internal evidence of Scripture, including a count of the number of Passovers in John, suggests that three and a half years is about right. This means that Jesus must have conducted his ministry sometime between about A.D. 26 and A.D. 33.

Now, our next task is to find a year when Nisan 15 fell on a Friday. In this general time period—from the late A.D. 20s to the early 30s— only four dates emerge as possible candidates for the Crucifixion (and by implication, the Resurrection):

- Friday, April 11, A.D. 27;
- Friday, March 18, A.D. 29;
- Friday, April 7, A.D. 30; and
- Friday, April 3, A.D. 33.

Finding exact correlations between our dates and the particular day in the month of Nisan is not always easy because setting the Jewish calendar—which was a lunar calendar—was sometimes as much of an art as a science. The first day of the month was supposed to begin when the new moon was *observed* by two witnesses and reported to the proper officials. So if a night happened to be cloudy, the first day of the month might have to be postponed for a day.

Even with these caveats in mind, all four of the above dates appear to have fallen on either Nisan 14 or Nisan 15. Furthermore, according to George B. Caird of Oxford, who has been recognized as a leading authority in researching this issue, the third candidate—Friday, April 7, A.D. 30—is the front-runner.

Probably the first date in A.D. 27 is too early, given the most likely times for Jesus' birth and the start of his ministry. The other two dates— A.D. 29 and A.D. 33—are possibilities, but for a number of technical reasons, they have been discarded. So most scholars have settled on the A.D. 30 date.

Issue #3: The Length of Time in the Tomb

Finally, some people worry that the dating of the Resurrection may be thrown off by the requirements of prophecy, including Jesus' own predictions, that he spend three days in the tomb.

On the face of it, these critics say, if he was buried on Friday afternoon and if he rose early Sunday morning, that would give him only about a day and a half in the tomb. The problem, as these concerned readers see it, is that Jesus should have spent three *full* days in the tomb to fulfill the various prophecies he gave during his ministry (see Matt. 16:21, 17:23, 20:19).

So should we move the date of the Crucifixion backward, or the date of the Resurrection forward, to ensure that Jesus had a full three days in the tomb?

It is quite true that by the traditional reckoning we have been following up to this point, Jesus would have spent only about thirty-six hours in the tomb—not the seventy-two hours covered by three full days. In other words, he would have been buried just before sundown on Friday. Then, he would have been in the tomb all day Saturday. Finally, he would have risen from the dead early Sunday morning.

Assume, for instance, that he was buried at 5:00 P.M. on Friday and was raised at 5:00 A.M. on Sunday. That would mean his body was in the tomb only thirty-six hours.

There are a couple of reasonable responses to such concerns. First, Jesus usually says he would be raised up "*on* the third day." This means that it would be *impossible* for a full seventy-two hours to elapse because the third day could not have ended if he was raised on it.

Second, in the first century, a common way of calculating the passage of several consecutive days was to count part of a day as one day. For that matter, we often make use of the same convention in our own day. You might say, for instance, "I visited such-and-such a client on Thursday and Friday." But that doesn't necessarily mean you spent all of both days with that client. You may have spent only an hour or two one day and a similar amount of time the next day.

So when we translate this way of thinking to the Resurrection, we arrive at this conclusion: Jesus was buried during a short part of the first day (Friday), all of the second day (Saturday), and part of the third day (Sunday). In our own common parlance, he would have been in the tomb "three days"—even though he didn't spend a full seventy-two hours there.

Even the statement by Jesus in Matthew 12:40 that he would be in the heart of the earth "three days and three nights" can be resolved rather easily. The reason is that an alternative way of referring to a day in first-century times was to call it "a day and a night"—even if a whole day or night hadn't actually expired.

Expressions in our own day may also reflect a similarly loose understanding of "night." For example, you might say, "I had to work all night on this report," but that doesn't necessarily mean you failed to get any sleep. In fact, you may really mean you worked several hours after dinner—an unusual practice for you—and then you went to bed a little later than normal.

Or perhaps you have said, "That was a short night," on occasions when you went to bed very late and then had to get up very early. Or maybe you bade "good night" to someone who was retiring very early—even though the sun hadn't yet set. Even the Beatles, in their hit song, "A Hard Day's Night," helped popularize a broader understanding of how the words *day* and *night* might be used.

Journalists certainly prefer to be as precise as possible with their words, but they also recognize that there is a place for popular and common usage. The early church theologians and historians weren't bothered by this three-day issue—and we shouldn't be either.

The Final "When"

Now, let's sum up where we are on this "when" question.
- Jesus was crucified and buried on Friday, April 7, A.D. 30.
- He was raised from the dead early Sunday morning, April 9, A.D. 30.

With these two dates settled, the rest is easy. We know from Acts 1:3 that Jesus spent forty days making his resurrection appearances, and then he ascended into heaven. This means that the Ascension took place on May 19, A.D. 30.

With the "what," "who," and "when" questions answered, we are ready to move on to the next major issue, which can get stickier than you might think at first. I'm referring to the challenges posed by the "where" of the Resurrection.

CHAPTER 9

The "Where" Question— A Resurrection Travel Guide

The dateline for the rewrite in chapter 5 is "Jerusalem"—and that certainly is where the resurrection story begins. But the "where" question for the greatest news story of all time takes us far beyond this first-century city.

The geographical range of the Resurrection moves swiftly from the narrow confines of one obscure tomb, to various places in the vicinity of Jerusalem, to the Sea of Galilee, and finally to another dimension of reality as open-ended as eternity itself. Even though we begin at the empty tomb, we soon find ourselves standing with eyewitnesses, gazing up into the heavens toward a destination that is well beyond our familiar realm of space and time.

Now, let's begin our exploration of the "where" of this story by focusing on the location of the first event—the tomb of Jesus Christ.

The Quest for the True Tomb

Where did it all begin? The resurrection reporters give us these facts about the tomb:

- The tomb was "outside the gate" but "near the city" of Jerusalem at Golgotha, the "Place of the Skull," where Jesus was crucified (see John 19:16–20; Heb. 13:12).
- The tomb was in a garden (John 19:41).
- The tomb, a new gravesite that had never been used before, was donated by a secret follower of Jesus, Joseph of Arimathea. In fact, Joseph had constructed the tomb for himself (Matt. 27:60).
- The tomb was "cut into the rock" (Luke 23:53 NASB), and a "rolling stone" was placed before the entrance (Mark 15:46).
- The entrance to the tomb was placed so that the resting place for the body (the loculus) could be seen by someone like John, who peered into the tomb and saw the linen burial wrappings—but without actually entering the sepulcher (see John 20:5).
- The inside of the tomb was large enough to allow several people to stand up and converse, as the women and the two angels did in Luke 24:1–8.
- The tomb may have been located in rolling or hilly terrain, perhaps in the side of a hill or upslope. In any event, it must have been situated so that viewers could sit and look at it, perhaps by

leaning back against another rock or slope of ground (see Matt. 27:61 [NASB], where Mary Magdalene and the "other" Mary sit "opposite" the tomb as Joseph of Arimathea and Nicodemus bury Jesus).

These, then, are the bare facts we have to work with in our quest for Jesus' tomb. No road map has been passed down to guide us to the exact site.

But what we do have, after centuries of searching, is two leading candidates: The first is the more ancient choice, which lies under the present-day Church of the Holy Sepulchre in the "Old City" of Jerusalem. The second is a more recent selection, known as the "Garden Tomb," just outside the walls of the Old City.

The Ancient Choice: The Church of the Holy Sepulchre

In about A.D. 326, the first Church of the Holy Sepulchre was ordered built by the Roman emperor Constantine the Great, who was converted to Christianity in A.D. 312. A few years earlier, an ancient tomb had been uncovered at this site, which by a long tradition had been regarded as the place where Jesus was crucified and buried.

Some have questioned the authenticity of the tradition because nearly three centuries had passed, with considerable turmoil, confusion, and violence. By the time ground was broken for the church, Jerusalem had been sacked; Herod's temple had been destroyed; the Jewish Christians in the area had scattered to other lands; and a pagan temple had been erected over the site.

Furthermore, since the original church was dedicated in A.D. 336, it has been destroyed and restored several times. The present structure dates back only to the year A.D. 1810.

Today, visitors to the Church of the Holy Sepulchre may be puzzled or even repelled when they approach the building, which lies in the middle of the northwestern area of the Old City, surrounded by shops and crowds. The first thing that may concern a pilgrim who is familiar with the biblical accounts of the burial of Christ is that the present-day church is clearly *within* the walls of Old Jerusalem. On its face, this fact would seem to disqualify the site as a possibility for the tomb of Jesus. Remember, according to Scripture, the tomb lay *outside* the gates.

I can still remember the trouble I had finding the church. When I finally located it and made my way past the trinkets and souvenirs being sold in the bazaar outside, I had to squeeze past hordes of other tourists going in and out of the sanctuary.

The scene inside was as disappointing as what I had encountered outside. First of all, the omnipresent candles, icons, marble overlays, and other decorations mostly obscured the impact of any archaeological evidence. Second, I sensed no inner feeling that "this is where the greatest event in history happened!"

Still, even though I experienced no emotional impact during this visit, I had to concede that the Church of the Holy Sepulchre does have several strong points in its favor.

First, the archaeological findings provide us with evidence that makes it possible to reconcile the Bible with the Holy Sepulchre site. The British archaeologist, Dame Kathleen M. Kenyon, along with a number of other experts, has concluded that in Jesus' time, the gravesite at the Holy Sepulchre actually lay outside the city walls. It was only after Herod Agrippa built an additional wall on the north side of the city in A.D. 41–44 that the tomb was encompassed by the walls (see *Digging Up Jerusalem*, pp. 226–235).

Of course, the argument for the Church of the Holy Sepulchre does not become decisive just because the site there lay outside the Jerusalem walls in A.D. 30. Nor is it conclusive that there happened to be an ancient grave in the same location.

But when you add in the long-standing tradition that has linked Jesus' burial to this particular spot, the arguments by the site's supporters become more convincing. In fact, the site has been generally accepted since ancient times by several major Christian bodies, including the Roman Catholics, Greek Orthodox, Armenians, Syrians, Coptics, and Abyssinians.

Unfortunately, there is no way to determine whether the Church of the Holy Sepulchre meets many of the biblical requirements—such as being in a garden, being large enough for several people to stand up in, and having an entrance positioned so that someone on the outside could look in and see the burial ledge without actually entering.

On the other hand, a second candidate for Christ's tomb—which has become quite popular in recent years with other Christian groups, especially certain Protestants and Evangelicals—can meet all of these requirements. This is the site commonly known as the "Garden Tomb."

The Recent Discovery: The Garden Tomb

The Garden Tomb gets its name from John 19:41, which refers to the presence of a garden at the place where Jesus was crucified and buried. This site began to intrigue some Christians in the late nineteenth century when it was linked to "Gordon's Calvary."

Gordon's Calvary is a rocky, skull-like formation, just across the street from the northern Jerusalem wall, between the Damascus Gate and Herod's Gate. The site was identified by the nineteenth-century British general Charles George Gordon—who was known as "Chinese Gordon" and "Gordon of Khartoum" from his foreign military exploits.

Gordon became convinced in 1883 that this spot was the true location of the Crucifixion. The nearby Garden Tomb, which had been discovered earlier, in 1867, soon became associated with Gordon's site. By 1894, the Garden Tomb Association had been established in London to provide funds to purchase the entire site and refurbish it.

Today, the Garden Tomb and Gordon's Calvary have become a meditative oasis in the middle of a loud, bustling metropolitan area. Located a short walk from the Damascus Gate of the Old City to the north along Nablus Road, this site, set in a restful garden, contrasts sharply with the hullabaloo around the Church of the Holy Sepulchre. The two-room cave that constitutes the tomb was cut out of rock, and has been dated by archaeologists back at least to the time of Christ. There is also a space for a "rolling stone" just outside the entrance.

Like the apostle John, visitors must bend over to enter the tomb. But once inside, they find the space seems almost to resemble a tiny apartment. The first room is empty, but was large enough to accommodate fifteen members of one group of Americans who crowded into the space and began to sing gospel songs during one visit I made there.

The second small room, situated just to the right of the first, is "furnished" in such a way that it's impossible to miss its purpose. On one side, a burial ledge has been hewn out of the rock, with a "pillow" fashioned out of the stone at one end, and a place for the feet at the other. Across this second room is another, unfinished burial ledge.

When I first saw the Garden Tomb, I fully intended to examine the site analytically. The questions rattling around in my head were more logical than emotional—a typical approach for a skeptical reporter:

- "Is this site really a convincing candidate for Jesus' tomb?"
- "Outward trappings aside, does the Garden Tomb truly seem more authentic than the Church of the Holy Sepulchre?"
- "If this is the real place, why wasn't it discovered earlier than a century ago?"
- "Is this just an attempt by Protestants and Evangelicals to distance themselves from groups like the Catholics and Orthodox churches?"
- "Is this merely another tourist attraction?"

But I must confess that my questions were quickly forgotten when I first set eyes on the entrance to the Garden Tomb . . . when I saw people stooping over at the entrance and looking in, much as the apostle John must have done on that first Easter morning . . . when I heard a group of Korean Christians standing near a burst of bright red flowers, singing "Near the Cross" in their own language.

Suddenly, I was hit head-on by wave after wave of emotion—perhaps some combination of that joy, fear, and awe that engulfed those first eyewitnesses, the first-century Christian women and men who saw the empty tomb and encountered the risen Christ.

When I tried to pose a question to one of the guides at the tomb, the words wouldn't come out. But the tears did.

"It's all right," he said to me. "This happens to most people, especially the first time they visit this place."

As my objectivity deserted me in that moment, I was struck by the realization that it is not the site that matters as much as the event.

Regardless of the merits of the arguments for one tomb location or the other, the important thing was not so much the "where" but the "who"—Christ himself—and the "what"—his resurrection.

So I remain attached emotionally to the Garden Tomb, mainly because of my own experience there. But I know it was more the Person than the place that made the difference.

In any event, the empty tomb, wherever it was, was only the starting point. From there, the risen Christ moved to other geographical locations throughout the Holy Land—and so did I, in the hope of tasting a bit of the excitement that he spread in those forty days before the Ascension.

Following the Risen Jesus

Today, only a few stones and foundations of the Jerusalem of Jesus' day remain visible in the Old City. In fact, the narrow, winding streets—though probably similar to those in ancient times—are about fifty to eighty feet above the thoroughfares of Jesus' day.

Still, as I walked—and sometimes jogged—along the Via Dolorosa, traditionally the street along which Jesus had dragged his cross toward Calvary, I received a strong impression of the difficult topography of the region. Jerusalem, which sits about 2,400 feet atop the Judean hills, is almost always "up," and no matter what road you take leading out of the city, you will be going "down."

This elevation has been recognized in verses like Acts 18:22, where Luke says that when Paul had "landed at Caesarea, he went *up* and greeted the church [at Jerusalem] and then went *down* to Antioch" (my emphasis).

Many of the witnesses to the risen Christ—such as Cleopas and his unnamed companion, who walked more than seven miles to Emmaus and then walked back the same day—must have had vigorous workouts. To get a feel for the physical challenge, I jogged early one morning over the Via Dolorosa, beginning at the Ecce Homo arch, which was built by the Roman emperor Hadrian in A.D. 135. This arch supposedly rises over the spot where Pilate had pointed to Jesus and said, "Behold the man" (John 19:5, KJV).

There were few people around as I headed "down" the narrow street. But then the slope of the ground changed dramatically as I started "up" on the next leg of the route.

The physical challenge hit me like a brick wall. Jogging upward at a thirty-degree angle through the narrow Jerusalem street, I began to breathe much harder than normal and was forced to shorten my stride considerably.

I could imagine that Jesus must have been wrestling with a nearly impossible physical burden as he struggled toward Golgotha. After all, he had been whipped, abused, deprived of sleep, and burdened with a heavy beam of wood on his back. It was amazing to me that he got as far as he did without the help of Simon of Cyrene.

And what a contrast it must have been after his resurrection, for him to cover this same ground in his risen body! Of course, in this risen state he could move from here to there in a flash, and appear and disappear at will.

Still, I found myself wondering, "Did the risen Christ, in his special, newly constituted body, *perspire* as I was doing? Did his legs become *fatigued*, or did he become *winded* on the road to Emmaus?"

It seems highly unlikely that he would have been subject to our limitations of endurance and stamina, given what we know about his remarkable resurrected body. After all, he was not limited as we are by our space-time reality. The open-ended "where" of Christ's post-resurrection condition must have struck him as totally different from the earthbound "where" of his preresurrection ministry.

On to Galilee

Just as his followers obeyed the instructions of the risen Jesus to meet him in Galilee, I headed north from Jerusalem. My goal: to experience as best I could the physical setting of the resurrection events in the north.

I spent several days around the large beautiful lake, the Sea of Galilee, or Sea of Tiberias, as it is sometimes called. This body of water may be as smooth and placid as glass one moment, or as stormy and choppy as an open sea the next.

Appropriately, the first site I looked for was that place on the northwestern seashore, where Jesus had built a cooking fire and then hailed Peter and six other disciples who were fishing about a hundred yards offshore.

By tradition, the site is located where the present Church of St. Peter (or Chapel of the Primacy) now stands. This little black basalt chapel was built by the Franciscans on the western shore in 1943. It's only a short walk from here to the traditional Mount of Beatitudes, and a couple of miles south of the ruins of Capernaum, Jesus' home base during his Galilean ministry.

As with many other biblical sites in Israel, there is considerable uncertainty about the authenticity of the location of the seaside encounter of Jesus with his disciples after his resurrection. But as early as the Middle Ages, pilgrims to the Holy Land revered this place as "Mensa Christi," or "Tabula Domini"—that is, "the table of Christ," or "the table of the Lord."

As I stood outside the chapel, at the edge of the calm sea with an occasional ripple washing up at my feet, it was easy to imagine that this was just the sort of place Jesus might have picked for his resurrection meeting with Peter, John, James, Thomas, Nathanael, and two other disciples.

I studied the story again in my pocket New Testament and meditated anew on the event. As you will recall from the resurrection rewrite, after Jesus had miraculously filled the disciples' empty nets with fish, he served the fish and bread he had been preparing. Then, he launched into his discussion with Peter, asking the apostle three times if he loved him, and telling him three times to feed or tend to his sheep.

Perhaps that early morning event nearly two thousand years ago had occurred on just such a still, cool day. Yet as I read, I could feel in my own gut the tension that must have been building up in Peter as he kept trying to answer Jesus' questions—but discovered that his master was looking for something more.

But now, the time had arrived to move on. So I began the ten- to fifteen-minute walk up the road to the traditional Mount of Beatitudes.

On this spot, Jesus may well have delivered the Sermon on the Mount, and later, after his death and Resurrection, the Great Commission to the eleven apostles (Matt. 28:16-20).

The mount is a spacious, open, grassy slope punctuated by orange groves and crowned by a church and convent belonging to Italian Franciscan nuns. As I walked up, I could see why some Bible scholars believe that the resurrection appearance to more than five hundred believers, which Paul refers to in 1 Corinthians 15, may have taken place here. There is plenty of room for hundreds, even thousands to stand or sit comfortably—such as the five thousand people Jesus fed with the five loaves and two fishes. (In fact, the Church of the Multiplication, which commemorates that event, is located only a short distance from this mount.)

But of course, Jesus did not just minister in the countryside or in rural communities. Many of his most important teachings—and certainly the two most important events in his life, the Crucifixion and the Resurrection—occurred in an urban setting. That may well be why, after he had finished his other resurrection travels, he returned to Jerusalem.

Returning to Jerusalem

The final event in the resurrection drama took place on the Mount of Olives, which lies just across the Kidron Valley, to the east of Jerusalem and the Temple Mount. So upon returning to Jerusalem, I retraced the possible path of Jesus and his apostles, as they walked from the city on the fortieth and last day of his appearances.

I chose the early morning for my final jog, to ensure relatively few people would be in the area. The air was cool and crisp, and the sky was clear, with stars and moon still on the horizon.

My destination was a place that has been designated as the "Garden of Gethsemane," just a couple of miles down the road on the lower part of the same slope where the traditional Mount of Olives is located. I really didn't expect to find the gates to this site open that early, but I decided to give it a try.

So I ran eastward along the northern Jerusalem wall from the Damascus Gate, past Herod's Gate, and down a steep incline into the Kidron Valley. The only person I encountered was an old Arab on a donkey, who was urging his animal up the hill toward me.

To my surprise the gate to the Garden of Gethsemane was open—though it was long before the regular tourist hours. Pleased that I might have the entire place to myself, I slipped inside and sat on a bench for several minutes of prayer and meditation.

A short distance away, I could see ancient olive trees, which were said to be more than two thousand years old. Perhaps they, like the stones around and under them, had actually been there at the very time that Jesus and his disciples had walked on these slopes. What events they must have seen, and what teachings they must have heard!

As I looked further up on the slope, I realized that somewhere nearby, Jesus said his final farewell to the eleven apostles.

Then, as they watched him ascend into the heavens, the two angelic figures appeared and, in effect, said, "He'll come again, in just the same way!"—the strong implication being that it was time to stop standing around. The disciples had to get ready because an entirely new and challenging phase of their ministry was about to begin.

With the Ascension, the "where" of the Resurrection Report comes to a close. Of course, we could speculate about where Jesus went after he returned to the Father—and what heaven might be like. But that's another story, and we still haven't finished with the one we are investigating.

You see, any good journalist, after covering the "who," "what," "when," and "where," will always move on to explore the "how"—and if possible, even the "why."

These are our last two stops: first the "how" and then the "why" of the Resurrection.

CHAPTER 10

The "How" Question— The Secret of the Tomb

Since the beginning of Christian history, there has always been an assumption that the tomb of Jesus Christ was empty on that first Easter morning.

None of the earliest Christian writers, heretics, or opponents of the faith have even suggested that Jesus' body stayed there in the tomb, where Joseph of Arimathea and Nicodemus buried it just after the Crucifixion. In fact, as we have already seen in our discussions of Matthew's report on the Resurrection, even the religious authorities accepted the guards' reports that the tomb was empty. That's why they invented their story about the disciples' stealing the body.

On the other hand, one of the most provocative, fascinating, and controversial questions that has been raised about the Resurrection focuses on the gravesite: "How did the tomb become empty on that first Easter morning?"

Many attempts have been made to answer this question, both by believers and nonbelievers. As a journalist dealing with this subject, I have been fascinated by some of the convoluted, irrational arguments that have emerged. In many cases, they would be laughed out of any newsroom—and the reporter offering them would be told to find a more credible explanation, or return to journalism school.

Now, let's consider first some of the skeptics' arguments and objections as to how the tomb became empty. Then we'll turn to some thoughts from more traditional Christians—and include an update on the research surrounding the curious case of the Shroud of Turin.

The Skeptics Attempt to Answer the "How" Question

U.S. Supreme Court Justice Antonin Scalia, speaking with sarcastic humor to a Jackson, Mississippi, audience in 1996, said: "The wise do not believe in the resurrection of the dead. It is really quite absurd. So everything from the Easter morning to the Ascension had to be made up by the groveling enthusiasts as part of their plan to get themselves martyred" (from an article in *The Washington Post*, quoted by the *Palm Beach Post*, April 10, 1996, p. 3A. The speech was delivered at an event sponsored by the Christian Legal Society and held at the Mississippi College School of Law.)

Justice Scalia rightly points up the absurdity of the notion that the early Christians would have made up a story about the Resurrection—

and then died for it. As a result, it's hard to find a reasonably intelligent nonbeliever who would begin an attack on Christianity by saying, "There was no empty tomb."

But even though most people, regardless of their beliefs, accept the fact that the followers of Jesus and their opponents found no body, that doesn't resolve the issue. Over the centuries, the skeptics have come up with a variety of nonmiraculous explanations for *how* this happened.

Here are just a few, which can also be found in popular or scholarly apologetic literature, such as the writings of John R. W. Stott, Leon Morris, and Josh McDowell.

The Disciples-Took-It Argument

According to this position—which is basically the same as the cover-up story that Matthew says the religious authorities settled upon—the disciples stole Jesus' body, hid it somewhere, and then went about preaching that he had risen from the dead.

This stratagem might have been believable if the disciples stood to gain money or some other concrete benefit from the deception. But what would be the payoff for the disciples? They had much more to lose than to gain: The Christian leaders who preached the gospel got in trouble with the local religious rulers, and they were sometimes tossed into prison (see Acts 4–5). Some were even executed (see Acts 12:1–2).

If the disciples had stolen the body, surely they would not have been willing to go through so much danger and discomfort for a lie. At some point, *someone* among their number would have tired of the deception and "come clean" about the story. When the body was finally identified or produced, the entire spiritual bubble that the early Christians were creating would have burst.

Also, there are related issues that make this an extremely weak argument. For example, how would the disciples have made it past the guards at the tomb? Even if the soldiers had fallen asleep, they would have awakened at the noise as the intruders moved the huge rolling stone and removed a body that weighed at least 250–300 pounds with the accompanying spices.

For obvious reasons, few skeptics are ready to make this argument about the empty tomb.

The Guards-Took-It Argument

There is an easy answer to this one: If the guards took the body, then why didn't they just produce it when the disciples began to preach about the risen Christ?

A major thrust of the church's message throughout Acts was the Resurrection, and this theme dominated parts of many of Paul's letters. Clearly, the preaching of a risen Messiah was a thorn in the side of the Jerusalem religious authorities. The best way to shut the mouths of the apostles would have been to bring out the body.

The Third-Party-Thieves-Took-It Argument

A variation on the first two arguments, this one may be the weakest. Again, the thieves would have had the challenge of getting through the guard, carting off the body, and leaving the site neat and clean.

Also, what would be the purpose of stealing the body? Grave robbers typically leave the bones and bodies alone and make off with any valuables at a gravesite. There would seem to be no financial benefit to taking the body—unless the thieves had some use for the spices that Nicodemus had packed in the grave clothes. But then why not just take the spices—and not the body?

This is three strikes for the skeptics, but being a tenacious lot, they are not "out" quite yet.

The Wrong-Tomb Argument

According to this theory, the women and other witnesses to the empty tomb, including Peter and John, became confused or couldn't see clearly in the early dawn hours—and so they went to the wrong tomb.

This other tomb was empty, and so they ran back and reported that Jesus had risen.

Now, we are moving into the realm of silliness. Even if some of the eyewitnesses lost their way that first Easter morning, it's inconceivable that *all* would have made the same mistake.

Also, what would stunned guards be doing outside an empty tomb? And again, if the disciples had run around claiming a resurrection that had never occurred, all the religious leaders would have had to do was go to the *real* tomb and stop their story in mid-stride.

The Unconscious-Christ Argument

This argument—also sometimes known as the "swoon theory"—says that Jesus was not dead when he was taken off the cross, but was just unconscious from his wounds. Then, when he was taken into the tomb and spices were applied, he revived and walked out. His resurrection appearances would have been in the flesh, not in a risen body.

There are so many flaws in this argument that it's hard to know where to begin. First, consider the severity of the wounds inflicted on him: from the flogging, to the crown of thorns, to the nails in the hands and feet on the cross, to the sword in the side.

An article in the prestigious *Journal of the American Medical Association*, which dealt in detail with the torture Jesus experienced, came to this conclusion: "Modern medical interpretation of the historical evidence indicates that Jesus was dead when taken down from the cross" (William D. Edwards, M.D., et al. "On the Physical Death of Jesus Christ," *JAMA*, March 21, 1986, pp. 1455–1463).

This research article should settle the issue, but let's take it a step further: Even if Jesus were not dead, when would he have revived and what would have been the consequences?

If he had revived when Nicodemus and Joseph of Arimathea were working on his body—and Mary Magdalene and the "other" Mary were looking on—their silence on the matter would make no sense. If they had already left and he revived, is it possible he could have rolled the heavy stone away from the inside all by himself and then escaped without the guards noticing? The whole scenario is far more unbelievable than a simple, supernatural resurrection.

Finally, if we assume that his "resurrection" appearances were really appearances in the still-living flesh, where did he go after he had faked the Ascension?

Clearly, there are many holes in this argument.

The Hallucination Argument

I mention this position only in passing because it is usually employed to explain the later resurrection appearances. In other words, the disciples were gripped by a kind of mass hysteria, an emotional and psychological force that caused them to think they were seeing the risen Christ, when they really weren't.

This approach isn't at all convincing when it is applied to the empty tomb, because hallucinations don't make bodies disappear. If they began to preach and cause trouble as a result of their hallucinations, the religious authorities would have moved quickly to pull out the body and end their disruptive behavior.

The Legend-Myth Argument

From the vantage point of nearly two thousand years after the event, many nonbelieving theologians and philosophers today apparently feel they don't need to deal seriously with the first-century reports of an empty tomb.

So, in the name of "modern" biblical scholarship, they have concluded that the entire resurrection scenario—not to mention the Incarnation, the miracles of Christ, and anything else that smacks of the supernatural—should be rejected as fact. Instead, these events must be taken as "myth" or "legend" or simply made-up stories by later writers.

When you read some of the conclusions of the so-called "Jesus Seminar," for example, you may be reminded of some half-baked essay you wrote for your tenth-grade high school English class. First, let me introduce this "seminar."

Since 1985, a group of about seventy purported biblical scholars have been conducting highly publicized discussions about what words in the Gospels reflect the "real Jesus," and which ones are supposedly the result of later additions and editing. In their tome, *The Five Gospels: The Search for the Authentic Words of Jesus*, they present what they call the "Scholars' Version" of the four Gospels, plus a "Gospel of Thomas," which they regard as being just as authoritative as the traditional Gospels.

But "authoritative" is not really an appropriate word for their view of most of the New Testament texts. In this book, we have been accepting the resurrection reports and other parts of the New Testament at face value, just as we would any other newspaper or piece of historical writing. But the Jesus Seminar people seem intent on committing literary mayhem on the Gospels.

Their modus operandi is a four-color grading system for words in the Gospels that refer to Jesus, or words that come from his mouth:

- Red means he said it, or the passage definitely describes something real about Jesus.
- Pink means the scholars have reservations about the descriptive passages or the words of Jesus, but they will accept them tentatively as authentic.
- Gray means they might use some of the content, but they would not include the material in their database to determine who Jesus really was.
- Black means they would not include the passage about Jesus in the primary database. Furthermore, if the words are a direct quote from Jesus, black means he didn't say it. Or as one member put it, black for his quotes means "There's been some mistake" (see pp. 36–37).

How do the resurrection narratives fare under the standards laid down by the Jesus Seminar?

Every passage and quote from Christ is in black. This means that the members of this group think the entire resurrection story—including the empty tomb—is total fiction.

An explanation inserted after the appearance of Jesus to the seven disciples on the shores of the Sea of Galilee in John 21:1–14 is typical of their approach: "The dialogue assigned to Jesus in this account is the result of the storyteller's imagination," the scholars say (p. 468).

Now, I *think* I have been reading the same material that these Jesus Seminar people have. But try as I may, I can find no reasonable authority or signals in the biblical text to support their approach to reading Scripture.

Their hermeneutic (or principle of biblical interpretation) seems to go like this:

- Treat the Bible differently from all other works of ancient non-fiction by assuming that it is totally unreliable. So Herodotus, Thucydides, and Caesar's *Gallic Wars* are reasonably good historical sources—but the New Testament is not.
- Assume that the supernatural realm doesn't exist—or at least that the New Testament doesn't picture it accurately.
- Assume that most New Testament passages—and especially the resurrection narratives—are fiction.
- Rewrite the Bible at will by making up stories to explain away the clear words of Scripture.

Overall, these scholars do have academic credentials. But their interpretations and conclusions appear to be rooted more in personal fabrication and opinion than in hard fact. Remarkably, their color-coding has apparently put them in the position of rejecting even the existence of an empty tomb—at least if their "Scholars' Version" of the Bible is to be taken at face value.

The common thread in each of the above arguments for a non-miraculous answer to the empty tomb's "how" question is simply an unwillingness to accept a supernatural solution as a possibility. Remember our "strange" Rule of Reporting #13, which in effect says that an extradimensional explanation for an event can never be acceptable to a secular journalist. Apparently, this rule is followed implicitly not only by many reporters, but also by the average skeptic and nonbelieving theologian.

Unfortunately, once we close our minds to the spiritual realm, we can never see it, even when it hits us right between the eyes. But if our minds remain open to the extradimensional, even the sky may pose no limit—as some other answers to the "how" question suggest.

How Believers Answer the "How" Question

The empty tomb doesn't present the believer with any of the concerns that confront the nonbeliever. The nonbeliever *must* come up with a rational explanation for the empty tomb, or he faces the uncomfortable prospect of having to reevaluate his own beliefs. The believer, on the other hand, sees that vacant slab, or loculus, in Joseph of Arimathea's tomb as a rock-solid confirmation of his faith.

So most believers really don't worry too much about *how* the tomb became empty. All they know is that Christ is risen—and the empty tomb supports that fact. But increasingly, scientific thinkers who really believe that the tomb was empty and that Jesus rose physically from the dead are proposing some new possibilities.

These scholars are not in any way suggesting that they can explain the empty tomb or the Resurrection in terms of contemporary science. But they are beginning to draw on the language and insights of modern physics and other scientific disciplines in an effort to help us grasp a little more clearly what may have happened in the tomb on that first Easter.

The Space-Time Question

Try making a couple of assumptions with me: First, assume that there is a reality beyond our three-dimensional world of height, width, and depth. Second, assume that Jesus Christ somehow entered that extradimensional reality on the first Easter morning.

If both these assumptions are correct, many scientists would say that the "how" of the empty tomb may have some connection to the post-Einstein concept of space-time. Although this is an abstract concept that is not easy to understand, the space-time idea may provide us with some of the best contemporary language available to understand the drama of the empty tomb.

Dr. Thomas F. Torrance, one of the world's leading Reformed theologians, won the Templeton Prize for Progress in Religion in 1978 for his work linking this kind of science and Christianity. In his *Space, Time and Resurrection*, Torrance notes that "space-time is a four-dimensional continuum inseparable from the matter and energy of the universe . . . bound up with the speed of light which is of such a velocity that our senses cannot cope with it" (pp. 186–87).

In other words, Einstein helped add the important dimension of time to scientific reality. This means the three-dimensional space we occupy can't be seen as a static container of life. Rather, the space you now occupy as you sit, reading these lines, should be regarded as always changing in the lightning-fast forward movement of time. The past has disappeared, and the future has yet to appear, but they are both no less real than the present.

Torrance goes on to observe that the "space-time continuum is necessarily invisible. This means that we must penetrate beyond the immediate and crude observation of things into the inherently non-observable structure of the space-time framework of the universe, if we hope to grasp reality."

As for the Resurrection, Torrance warns that we "must not be misled into thinking that such an event as the resurrection may be 'explained' or made 'intelligible' simply in terms of the invisible structures of space-time" (p. 187). The reason for our limitations, he says, is that we are not only dealing with space-time, but with *God's intervention* in space-time.

Still, Torrance feels that "the only acceptable account" of the Resurrection must make use of some of the post-Einstein thinking and terminology. If we continue to explore this area, he says, we might reach an entirely new understanding of the empty tomb through laws of physics that may have been involved in Christ's Resurrection.

In lay terms, what Torrance seems to be suggesting is this: When Jesus rose from the dead, and when he made appearances to his disciples through closed doors, his resurrection body was caught up in light-speed-fast invisibility that may characterize accelerated movement through space and time.

In other words, in his resurrection body, the risen Christ was operating according to "natural" laws. But he was doing so in ways that a human being who has never been resurrected cannot imagine.

This is heady stuff for a down-to-earth news reporter. But those on the science beat, during their coverage of stories about breakthroughs in theoretical physics, have been exposed to some of the strange and exciting possibilities of space-time. As a result, they may be in a better position than most of us to grasp the sophisticated physics that could have been involved in the empty tomb phenomenon.

But physicists aren't the only scientists who have been exploring what happened in the tomb of Christ. Another issue—the possible survival of the burial cloth of Christ—has drawn scientists from a variety of disciplines into an ongoing controversy that always seems to begin anew, just as it seems resolved.

The Curious Case of the Shroud of Turin

The Shroud of Turin is a piece of cloth that just won't slip quietly out of sight and mind.

There are various claims that the shroud, which has been kept by Catholic officials in Turin, Italy, since the sixteenth century, was the burial wrapping for Christ. The first historical record of the shroud was in 1354, when it came into the possession of a famous French knight, Geoffroi de Charnay. Observers noticed a vague, reddish image of a man on the surface, and soon, the word spread that this was the burial shroud of Christ.

The cloth became quite controversial, as some church officials denounced it as a clever painting, and others revered it as the actual burial linen that had covered Jesus in the tomb.

The first dramatic scientific breakthrough in evaluating the shroud came in 1898, when a photographer, Secondo Pia, took photographs as the cloth hung above an altar. The developed photos, which were in black and white, were not as important as the negatives, which showed a clear image of a man who had all the marks of crucifixion. In other words, somehow, a negative image, like a photo exposure, had been created on the cloth.

The marks on the man's body, which were now quite clear, seemed consistent with the description in the Bible of the torture and crucifixion of Jesus. In 1902, Yves Delage, a professor of comparative anatomy at the Sorbonne, analyzed Pia's photos and concluded that the picture of the body and the nature of the wounds were anatomically accurate.

Various other tests have been performed on the shroud at different points in the twentieth century, but the most devastating for those who believe in the authenticity of the cloth was the radiocarbon testing done in 1988. The conclusions of this test were that the cloth of the shroud was produced in the Middle Ages, between A.D. 1260 and 1390. The Roman Catholic church accepted this finding and declared the shroud inauthentic, but still worthy of veneration because of the image of Christ on it.

For many people, this test settled the matter—until reports surfaced about research being conducted by two microbiologists, Dr. Leoncio A. Garza-Valdes and his colleague Dr. Stephen J. Mattingly from the University of Texas at San Antonio. These scientists, building on work that Dr. Garza-Valdes had done with the shrouds of mummies, determined that the carbon 14 tests on the Shroud of Turin were flawed.

Specifically, the scientists found that a tiny piece of the shroud, which Garza-Valdes secured from Catholic authorities in Turin, was covered with "biogenic varnishes," or plastic-like coatings synthesized by bacteria or fungi. This meant that the carbon tests had actually measured the age of the outer coating, or varnish, of the linen, and not the linen itself.

Dr. Garza-Valdes is in the process of trying to get permission from the Vatican to do further tests on the shroud, but so far he has been unsuccessful. Still, preliminary observations have suggested to him that, given the build-up of the varnishes, the actual age of the cloth could go back to the time of Christ.

"I have found no reason why the Shroud of Turin cannot be the burial cloth of Jesus of Nazareth," Dr. Garza-Valdes says.

* * * * *

Where will the checkered history of the shroud go from here?

Only further scientific testing can tell. In the meantime, no one, probably not even the shroud's most ardent supporters, would suggest that one's faith should depend on a physical object.

If additional testing does reveal solid support for a first-century date, that may provide evidence to confirm the convictions of some believers, and even prompt a few more skeptics to consider the meaning of the empty tomb.

But scientific measurements can never unveil the final secret of the tomb—the ultimate "how" that explains precisely what happened in that rock-hewn cavity on the first Easter. That secret will remain hidden, only to be revealed at some undetermined time in the future and perhaps in another dimension of reality—though we may gain some insights as we contemplate the "why" of the Resurrection.

CHAPTER 11

The "Why" Question— And Some Reflections on Miracles

Some reporters never get around to asking the "why" question, and even if they do, the subject matter doesn't always lend itself to an answer.

In some respects, the Resurrection Report is one of those stories that will always remain just beyond our grasp, just outside our full comprehension. Yet the resurrection reporters have given us a number of clues that can at least point us toward some understanding of the "why" of this event.

I suppose it all begins with John 3:16, "For God so loved the world . . ."

The reporter John says that Jesus came into the world— but with a definite mission. He came to die. His death was no mistake, not the result of some cosmic slipup, but the central objective in the divine plan. He had to die, because somehow, a principle is stamped in the fundamental laws of the universe that disobedience to God and his laws demands a blood sacrifice to set things right. We exist in a state of disobedience or estrangement from God, and Jesus was chosen as the perfect, only acceptable substitute for us.

The site of his sacrifice was the cross, erected in that "Place of the Skull" just outside the gates of Jerusalem, which we know as Golgotha. But his mission didn't end on the cross, or in the garden nearby, where he was buried in the tomb of Joseph of Arimathea, with one hundred pounds of myrrh and aloes packed about his body. Jesus said that he would rise on the third day, and he did.

Why did he rise? Why was that part of the plan?

The resurrection reporter John gives us one reason: "These [things] are written that you may believe that Jesus is the Christ, the Son of God, and that by believing you may have life in his name" (John 20:31).

So he rose in the first instance to help us believe in him. Being merely human, we might not have been impressed if he had just died—and if we had seen no evidence that he had been transported to be with the Father.

Paul put it quite well when he speculated on what his own response might have been if there had been no Resurrection: "If Christ has not been raised, your faith is futile; you are still in your sins. . . . If only for this life we have hope in Christ, we are to be pitied more than all men" (1 Cor. 15:17, 19).

Paul was not just interested in the here and now. He was not enamored of the things he could see, taste, and touch. He wanted more, much more. He wanted the kingdom of God, and all that he sensed might go with it.

Later in his first letter to the church at Corinth, he said:

> I declare to you, brothers, that flesh and blood cannot inherit the kingdom of God, nor does the perishable inherit the imperishable. Listen, I tell you a mystery: we will not all sleep, but we will all be changed. . . . When the perishable has been clothed with the imperishable, and the mortal with immortality, then the saying that is written will come true: 'Death is swallowed up in victory. Where, O death, is your victory?/Where, O death, is your sting?' (1 Cor. 15:50–51, 54–55)

The "why" of the Resurrection for Paul, then, is that the cross and the empty tomb are part of an eternal package, a promise that encompasses being reconciled to God *and* enjoying his company forever.

The British scholar and Christian apologist C. S. Lewis has noted that the Resurrection is the central theme in every sermon delivered in Acts. In his classic work *Miracles*, he goes on to say:

> He is the "first fruits," the "pioneer of life." He has forced open a door that has been locked since the death of the first man. He has met, fought, and beaten the King of Death. Everything is different because He has done so. This is the beginning of the New Creation: a new chapter in cosmic history has opened. (p. 145)

So for Lewis, as well as for Paul, the Resurrection was not just a point-in-time event, a historical oddity that we can analyze and argue about. Rather, Jesus' rising from the dead was the beginning of a new reality—a reality in which we can participate now, and celebrate throughout eternity.

The "why" of the Resurrection, then, is a deeply personal question, and the responses that have been offered come from deep within:

- Jesus rose so that you and I might begin *right now* to start tasting the same life that he enjoys so fully with the Father.
- He rose that we might experience that hope that reaches well beyond wishful thinking.
- And he rose that eventually we might enter into another reality—one that surpasses all our earthbound expectations and dreams.

If all this is true—and there is strong evidence that it is—the debates must end, and the Resurrection must indeed be accepted as the best news of all time.

ACKNOWLEDGMENTS

During the past twenty-five years, I have had the opportunity to speak thousands of times at Bible study classes, church worship services, college assemblies, retreats for clergy and laity, writers' seminars and conferences, and a variety of other gatherings. A substantial number of those appearances has been linked in some way to the Resurrection of Jesus Christ, either as direct teachings on the events involved in the Resurrection, or on related biblical topics.

As a result of preparing for and delivering these talks, I have become increasingly convinced, as the apostle Paul says, that the Christian faith is a useless, meaningless exercise if Jesus did not indeed rise from the dead. The Resurrection is, indeed, the central event of the gospel message. If Christ did not conquer death—if the message of the resurrection reporters was essentially a pack of lies—then why are we spending time in worship, prayer, study, and service, all in the name of Christ?

This book is certainly not intended as a "proof" of the Resurrection events, because ultimately, that must be a matter of faith and basic assumptions. But my own spiritual experiences—

and what I have heard from the many believers and searchers I have encountered over the past couple of decades—have convinced me that it's important to make the Resurrection as understandable, compelling, and believable as humanly possible.

Faith may transcend reason, but at the same time, faith is certainly not irrational, or against reason. Properly understood, the Resurrection and its aftermath are prime examples of just how plausible and reasonable the Christian faith is.

To this end, I have concentrated in this book on evaluating the Resurrection in light of the skeptical, tough-minded, rationalistic tools and methodology of my trade as a working journalist. As one colleague told me, if the Resurrection can stand up to this kind of analysis, it can stand up to anything.

But I have not reached this point entirely on my own. Although I absolve them of responsibility for any mistakes or conclusions in this book, I am deeply grateful to a number of people for their help in reading and critiquing this book from a variety of different scholarly perspectives and life experiences. These colleagues include Matthew Cox, Stuart Woodward, Chris Osborne, Ferd Becker, Doug McEvoy, Bill Gordon, David Fuller, Jim Vaughan, Grant Powell, and my wife and fellow writer, Pam Proctor.

The staffs at the Indian River County Main Library in Vero Beach, Florida, and at the Indian River Community College Library in Fort Pierce, Florida, have been quite helpful. In particular, Pat Profetta and Elaine Kromhout of Indian River Community College have made important books and other research materials available. In addition, Malcolm Murchison kindly supplied me with a number of scholarly texts.

Also, there are many pastors who have made it possible for me to conduct ongoing seminars and classes at their churches. A few include Ken Long at First Church of God in Vero Beach, Florida; Gordon MacDonald at Trinity Baptist in New York City (now at Grace Chapel in Lexington, Mass.); Keith Boyd at Trinity Baptist in New York City; Thomas Pike at St. George's Episcopal Church in New York City; and Philip A. C. Clarke at Park Avenue United Methodist Church in New York City.

In addition, I want to thank all those who have participated in my classes and other presentations at these churches. You have provided a kind of "hands-on laboratory" for me to fine-tune many of the concepts in this book—and to discard notions that were clearly off base.

Finally, I am grateful to Ken Stephens, the publisher at Broadman & Holman Publishers; to my editors, Leonard Goss and Matt Jacobson; to our editorial director, Bucky Rosenbaum; and to the rest of the editorial staff for giving me the opportunity and support to pursue this project. I trust that in some way, the hours that have gone into *The Resurrection Report* will pay off for you, the reader, in a better understanding of the greatest news story of all time.

William Proctor
Vero Beach, Florida

References

Analytical Greek Lexicon, The. Grand Rapids: Zondervan, 1977.

Barclay, William. *The Letters to the Corinthians*. Rev. ed. Philadelphia: Westminster, 1956.

Barrett, Jim. "Science and the Shroud." *The Mission* (University of Texas Health Science Center at San Antonio), spring 1996.

Boa, Kenneth and William Proctor. *The Return of the Star of Bethlehem*. Garden City, N.Y.: Doubleday, 1980.

Brady, John. *The Craft of Interviewing*. New York: Random House, Vintage Books, 1977.

Brown, Colin. *Miracles and the Critical Mind*. Grand Rapids: Eerdmans, 1984.

Brown, Raymond E. *The Gospel according to John XIII–XXI*, The Anchor Bible. Garden City, N.Y.: Doubleday, 1970.

Bruce, F. F. *Commentary on the Book of the Acts*. Grand Rapids: Eerdmans, 1980.

——. *The New Testament Documents: Are They Reliable?* Grand Rapids: Eerdmans, 1980.

Buttrick, George Arthur, ed. *The Interpreter's Dictionary of the Bible*. 4 vols. New York: Abingdon Press, 1962.

Cassels, Louis. *The Real Jesus: How He Lived and What He Taught*. Garden City, N.Y.: Doubleday & Company, 1968.

Cornfeld, Gaalyah, and David Noel Freedman. *Archaeology of the Bible: Book by Book*. San Francisco: Harper & Row, 1976.

Douglas, J. D., ed. *The New Bible Dictionary*. Grand Rapids: Eerdmans, 1962.

———— *The New International Dictionary of the Christian Church*. Grand Rapids: Zondervan, 1974.

Dowley, Tim, ed. *Eerdmans Handbook to the History of Christianity*. Grand Rapids: Eerdmans, 1977.

Edwards, William D., and others. "On the Physical Death of Jesus." *Journal of the American Medical Association* (1986): 1455–63.

Fallaci, Oriana. *Interview with History*. Boston: Houghton Mifflin, 1976.

Fuller, Reginald H. *The Formation of the Resurrection Narratives*. Philadelphia: Fortress Press, 1980.

Funk, Robert W., Roy W. Hoover, and the Jesus Seminar. *The Five Gospels: The Search for the Authentic Words of Jesus*. New York, Macmillan, 1993.

Gaeblein, Frank E., ed. *The Expositor's Bible*. Vols. 1, 8, 9, 10, and 12. Grand Rapids: Zondervan, 1979.

Geldenhuys, Norval. *Commentary on the Gospel of Luke*. Grand Rapids: Eerdmans, 1979.

Glaser, Mitch, and Zhava Glaser. *The Fall Feasts of Israel*. Chicago: Moody Press, 1987.

Grosheide, F. W. *Commentary on the First Epistle to the Corinthians*. Grand Rapids: Eerdmans, 1953.

Guthrie, D., and others, eds. *The New Bible Commentary*. Rev. ed. Grand Rapids: Eerdmans, 1975.

Kantzer, Kenneth. *Evangelical Roots*. Nashville: Thomas Nelson, 1978.

Kenyon, Kathleen M. *Digging Up Jerusalem*. London: Ernest Benn, 1974.

Lane, William L. *The Gospel according to Mark*. Grand Rapids: Eerdmans, 1978.

Lawes, D. N., and R. Moore, eds. *Fordor's Israel*. New York: David McKay Co., 1978.

Lewis, C. S. *Miracles: How God Intervenes in Nature and Human Affairs*. New York: Macmillan, 1960.

Lewis, Gordon, and Bruce Demarest, eds. *Challenges to Inerrancy: A Theological Response*. Chicago: Moody Press, 1984.

Lincoln, William C. *Personal Bible Study*. Minneapolis: Bethany Fellowship, 1975.

Marshall, I. Howard. *The Acts of the Apostles: An Introduction and Commentary*. Grand Rapids: Eerdmans, 1984.

———. *Luke: Historian and Theologian*. Grand Rapids: Zondervan, 1976.

Martin, Harold C. *The Logic & Rhetoric of Exposition*. New York: Rinehart & Co., 1958.

McBirnie, William Steuart. *The Search for the Tomb of Jesus*. Montrose, Calif.: Acclaimed Books, 1978.

McDowell, Josh, and Don Steward. *Answers to the Tough Questions Skeptics Ask about the Christian Faith*. San Bernardino, Calif.: Here's Life Publishers, 1980.

McDowell, Josh. *Evidence That Demands a Verdict*. San Bernadino, Calif.: Here's Life Publishers, 1979.

———. *More Evidence That Demands a Verdict*. San Bernardino, Calif.: Here's Life Publishers, 1980.

McGivena, Leo E. *The News: The First Fifty Years of New York's Picture Newspaper*. New York: News Syndicate Co., 1969.

Mencher, Melvin. *News Reporting and Writing*. 5th ed. Dubuque, Iowa.: William C. Brown Publishers, 1991.

Morison, Frank. *Who Moved the Stone?* Grand Rapids: Zondevan, 1958.

Morris, Leon. *The First Epistle of Paul to the Corinthians: An Introduction and Commentary*. Grand Rapids: Eerdmans, 1975.

———. *The Gospel according to John*. Grand Rapids: Eerdmans, 1977.

———. *The Gospel according to Luke*. Grand Rapids: Eerdmans, 1975.

New Encyclopaedia Britannica. 15th ed. Chicago: Encyclopaedia Britannica, 1989.

New International Version Interlinear Greek-English New Testament, edited and translated by Alfred Marshall. Grand Rapids: Zondervan, 1976.

One Year Chronological Bible, The. Wheaton, Ill.: Tyndale House, 1995.

Pirovolos, Nick. *Too Mean to Die*. Wheaton, Ill.: Tyndale House, 1982

Proctor, William. "A Reporter Looks at the Resurrection." *Christian Herald*. April 1980, 30–34.

———. "Running Where Jesus Walked." *Christian Herald*, April 1979, 28–32.

————. *The Templeton Touch*. Garden City, N.Y.: Doubleday, 1983.

Rivers, William L. *The Mass Media: Reporting—Writing—Editing*. New York: Harper & Row, 1966.

Robertson, A. T. *A Harmony of the Gospels for Students of the Life of Christ*. New York: Harper & Row, 1922.

Rosen, Ceil and Moishe Rosen. *Christ in the Passover: Why Is This Night Different?* Chicago: Moody Press, 1978.

Shroud of Turin home page. http://www.cais.net/npacheco/shroud/turin.hrml

Stott, John R. W. *Basic Christianity*. Grand Rapids: Eerdmans, 1983.

Strong, James. *The New Strong's Complete Dictionary of Bible Words*. Nashville: Thomas Nelson, 1996.

Strunk, William Jr., and E. B. White. *The Elements of Style*. New York: Macmillan, 1965.

Tasker, R. V. G. *The Gospel according to St. John: An Introduction and Commentary*. Grand Rapids: Eerdmans, 1978.

Torrance, Thomas F. *Space, Time and Resurrection*. Grand Rapids: Eerdmans, 1976.

Vilnay, Zev. *The Guide to Israel*. Jerusalem: Daf-Chen Press, 1978.

Wilcox, Robert K. *Shroud*. New York: Bantam Books, 1978.

Wilson, Ian. *The Shroud of Turin: The Burial Cloth of Jesus?* Garden City, N. Y.: Doubleday, 1978.

Zinsser, William. *On Writing Well*. 5th ed. New York: HarperCollins, 1994.

Index